The Kingdom *of* Surfaces

Also by Sally Wen Mao

Mad Honey Symposium
Oculus

The Kingdom *of* Surfaces

poems

Sally Wen Mao

Graywolf Press

This publication is made possible, in part, by the voters of Minnesota through a Minnesota State Arts Board Operating Support grant, thanks to a legislative appropriation from the arts and cultural heritage fund. Significant support has also been provided by the McKnight Foundation, the Amazon Literary Partnership, and other generous contributions from foundations, corporations, and individuals. To these organizations and individuals we offer our heartfelt thanks.

Published by Graywolf Press
212 Third Avenue North, Suite 485
Minneapolis, Minnesota 55401

www.graywolfpress.org

Published in the United States of America

ISBN 978-1-64445-237-0 (paperback)
ISBN 978-1-64445-238-7 (ebook)

2 4 6 8 9 7 5 3 1
First Graywolf Printing, 2023

Library of Congress Control Number: 2022946512

Cover design: Kapo Ng

Cover art: Ah Xian, *China, China–Bust 81*, 2004, glazed porcelain. Museum of Contemporary Art, gift of the artist, 2008. Image courtesy the artist and Museum of Contemporary Art Australia. Copyright © the artist. Photograph: Jenni Carter.

For Wu Juhua 吳菊華
my paternal grandmother, who became a poet in 2020

Here is one of her poems:

> 万里晴空满天明，
> 彩灯映照满城春。
> 黄鹤吐翠扬柳俏，
> 江水含情樱花红。
> 武汉古道游人织，
> 武昌寺院叩芳馨。
> 最佳春雨催时节，
> 普降甘霖万物生。

In memory of Tian Suzheng 田素贞
my maternal grandmother

Contents

兜

The Kingdom *of* Surfaces

Loquats

In the spring they ripen and swarm the trees,
the waxy little fruits that resemble bald heads.

I collect their remains: piebald, sweet
and sour. A syrup made of loquats

is said to cure cough. Their woolly twigs
splinter in pear blight. I am bereft

when I eat them all. My throat and heart
always sore. Whenever I got sick, my mother

used to skin yellow loquats, but they tasted
better with the skin on. This season, my cough

grows and grows. There is a tree or a fungus
in my chest. I once kissed a man in the hollow,

a tattoo of a tree stump on his chest. I counted
the rings to a hundred. His memory broke

against my cracked phone screen like waves
against the Sutro Baths. In different years

of my life, 2012 and 2017, two men
with the same name fucked me. Futility

was their name. Their bald heads, their kisses,
the spittle of spite, crawl into me, refusing to exit.

At the herbal medicine store, the most expensive
item is cordyceps or wormgrass, dead caterpillars

whose brains become host to a fungus that rots
them from the inside out. Good for the lungs,

a panacea for all pain, the saleswoman pitches.
I am wormgrass, expensive but brain-dead.

Comatose in my love, my refuse, futility fuels
my every waking hour. The tree inside me isn't loquat

but strangler fig. A tree so pretty and snakelike
it renders you breathless, then worthless, all at once.

On Porcelain

White fragility is priceless to the Empire
Porcelain is stronger, more translucent
than earthenware / The Chinese
invented porcelain back
around 200 BC
Recipe—kaolin,
feldspar, and
petuntse, heated
to 2,700 degrees in
a Jingdezhen kiln, spun

in whorls / A porcelain chimera
with the head of a serpent and body

of a lion sleeps in fire / Don't wake her up
She's a fire-breathing bitch / For millennia,

the West has attempted to replicate / Porcelain
and failed / Marco Polo tried to give it a name:
porcellana / As he presented a vase to his queen
Named for the translucent / White cowrie shell,
legal tender for the slave trade / A sister word to
porcella / Little hog / Its belly ripe for breeding,

for slaughter / After the French soldiers / Looted
Beijing's Old Summer Palace / They presented
their spoils to Empress Eugénie / After British
soldiers sacked the Old Summer Palace, they
presented their spoils / To Queen Victoria
When the British Royal Army handed
her a stolen Pekingese / Their queen
named the dog / Looty

Plunder is in the language of naming

My century of humiliation began with my body
To this day the cliché still stands: a white
woman's skin made of porcelain
At twelve, I collected
porcelain dolls,
all with blank European
complexions / Melancholia in pure
velvet capes and gingham summer dresses,
a hot fantasia / I was never taught to wish for
the features of these dolls, their rosy cheeks and tight
ringlets / I only learned that my face was flat and nothing
beautiful / That nothing beautiful can come from my blood,
my people / So when my first doll broke, her rosy cheek cracked

open / I collected shards, cut my fingers, cried as if my own cheek

was sliced open / In 1940 the Clarks conducted a psychological study

an experiment with dolls and children / Where did these babies learn

to hate themselves? they wondered / The value and delicacy of white

women, so priceless / A white woman's tears enough to burn Troy

In 1955, in Money, Mississippi, a white woman cries / And
the cost is a boy / Is Emmett / Is his mother weeping
at his casket / In 2020, in Central Park's north
woods / A white woman feigns distress,
calls the cops / On a Black man, a bird-
watcher / In this season of migration
Murder is in the language of her braying
If a white woman cries / Every tear reaps the sentence
My dolls / Their cheeks / Broken, the currency of innocence

Batshit

Say it. Say it to my face. Bat-eater, blood poacher. Carrier
       pigeon, germ-carrier, carrion breath, China virus,
filth, peril, pestilence, yellow jacket, yellow pest.

My teeth of pangolin scales, my mouth of death. Just because
       I have a mask on, doesn't mean I can't speak.

Doesn't mean I'm scared. Do you know how fast a virus kills
       a strong, healthy racehorse? In Australia, racehorses grazed
on grass full of bat droppings. That's how hundreds of horses dropped

dead, and their trainers died too. From bat shit. It's a shame
       how people die like their animals. How some love foreign
dogs more than foreign people. People petition against the lychee

and dog meat festival in Yulin—they call eating dog barbaric,
       but not police brutality. They hate a caged animal in a foreign
country, but ignore the border camps in their own.

Listen, I love dogs too. Here I am, wishing I had one,
       quarantined and hog-tied to solitude. When I go outside,
I wear sunglasses above my flu mask. It's not that I'm ashamed—

just last month, a woman was taking out the garbage
       in her tree-lined Brooklyn neighborhood, and someone
threw acid on her face, causing second-degree burns.

The difference between a monster and man's best friend
       is the difference between the lies you eat and the lies
you refuse to accept. Like that time a man lied

to me, I started crying and he called me hysterical.
       Which meant: batshit. Which meant:

Call me crazy, but bats signal good luck. In China, bats
        are a pun for blessing, good fortune. It's why emperors
and common folk alike had all their household objects

painted with clouds and flying bats—
        harbingers of another better world, these creatures living
upside down in perfect solitude, so still they are immortal.

Stolen several times in its lifetime, an imperial famille-rose
        porcelain vase with a pattern of bats and peaches, dogs
and lychees, sold at a Christie's auction

for $20 million. Enough to feed a village and supply
        its hospitals with N95 masks and respirators.

In Wuhan, it is daybreak and the field hospitals are closing.
        For months I worried about my family there, a city too far
away to raise alarm here in my home. Come April, some Americans

march against shelter-in-place. How worthless
        our bodies are to them, piling up in hallways and homes.

In America, bats are a portent of death. In the parks, under
        the sun, they swarm in broad daylight.
Vampire bats do not eat pollen or fruit. They have heat

        sensors near their nose that smell the warmth
of a racing heart. A single colony can drain twenty-five cows
        of blood. When you can't sleep, they hover near

your pulse. Hold your breath, turn on the lamp.
        Bathed in light, their wings flutter
                like heartbeats soon gone.

Wet Market

From youth I was taught that fresh meant alive
     until the moment you buy it   My mother
used to pick up chickens at the wet market,   slit the throats
herself   At four I helped her   defeather the fowl,
     drain its blood   in a vat

My parents barely ate meat   until the 1980s
     In reeducation camps,   they ate ground pork
once a year   In America, we don't buy   live chickens,
     but my mother always   wanted to see the fish
alive, head on before we took it   home

Scraps were the best sustenance—the eyes,   the head,
     the scales   At twelve I return   for the first time
to Wuhan   In the wet market, I touch live   snapping
     turtles, frogs in vats, smell the musk of   open-air
stalls   You want your meat squirming   and slippery,
not the squids and king conch   packed in ice

The butcher slices an eel in half—I squint   in disbelief
     at the dying I witness—live kill,   slit eel
Slit eyes, I've been called back home, my sightline   a bloodless
     gash   Wet markets flourish with produce,   feeding
a generation   Mine, the offspring   of those who starved,
     like my father,   in their mother's wombs

Now pundits call for their ban, citing   barbarian diets—
     raccoons, offal, civet   cats, bushmeat,
not spinach and wood ear,   plums and star apples
At the Berkeley farmers market, no one   bats
an eye How lovely it must be, to possess   a body cleaved of
     hunger and horrors, its stench so   inherently

clean   Nightly I dream of Angel Island's   quarantine
       station—my immigrant   body scrubbed
raw with carbolic soap, my immigrant   belongings fumigated
in sulfur steam The evening I saw death,   we ate eel braised
with bitter melon,   drowned it   in cloudy broth
       To this day the memory   how I tasted marrow
           like an elegy frozen   in bone

Cherry-Picking Season

My grandmother picks cherries
        like scabs. Sweetheart cherries,
                Rainier cherries,
        Coral, Lapins, Bing—
Late May: harvest time in Santa Cruz
        a red bounty in her palms. She gives
                us her offerings.
        As we split and pit them,
all that's left is perfect
        red flesh.
I wish we could harvest time.
        Days ago, the cardiologist broke:
        my grandmother harbors
                an abnormal growth
in her heart valves. The walls of her
        ventricles too hard,
each artery barklike. Anytime
                now, they will burst.
        My grandmother a tree
feeding all her children.
        What can we do? She's past eighty.
        After her hospital visit,
                she is dazed for days,
nursing a throb in her chest.
                So this is the end,
I hear her thinking. To live through famine,
        to give birth to three children
through these milkless, meatless years.
        Over breakfast she recalls
                how from 1959 to 1962
        she only ate fruit once.

A white cherry in her palm
                could pierce her heart,
      its taste lasting
on her tongue for months.
      Who are we
             without her? I chew
through every pit, expel them
      from my mouth
             like spit or hunger.

Solitary Generation

I have witnessed true love
        festoon my overpopulated city
                with trash, red contrails

My only child, your idleness
        amuses me, touches me
                on my scarred fingertips

In fields of magic, my history
        cannibalizes yours, your pointless
                daisies, your marjoram—

You grew up bored
        in gutted apartment complexes
                without allegiance

to any slogan or sound
        My leftover daughters, freezing
                your eggs in a tumbler

My bare-branched sons, fluffing
        your hens for the roost,
                I watched you kiss a tumbleweed

on the playground and it broke
        my heart   I wanted you to love
                yourself though I've never known

love myself, I can think of prettier
        things like a bag full of money
                abandoned on the platform

Daughter, swallow your wolfberries
      and abandon the cowhide handbag
            in a garbage bin sweet with rain

Son, don't idle away your muscle
      and become the half-bitten yuzu
            with its thread of fickle flies

Sunday Stroll through the Marriage Market

Old women kneel in the square with open umbrellas,
     their granddaughters pinned to the nylon.
          Osmanthus trees, summer-buttered,

torn—an August afternoon in the People's Park.
     Sky overcast, the pink Shanghai smog a heavy quilting
          for the scrawls, damp printouts

laminated, taped to each shelter:
     height, weight, measurements—*Woman. Born*
          1990. Raised here. Educated in London. Speaks

three languages. Virtuous. 1.60m. Hobbies—
     cooking. Playing with children. Flying kites. Virtue,
          the glint inside you turning dark.

Man. Born in 1981, Hangzhou. Good job
     at a banking firm. 175 cm tall. Needs a caring,
          devoted wife, preferably born in 1980s.

A strange man stares, asks you if you're "looking."
     You shake your head, *I'm just a tourist.*
          No, I am not alone. One truth, one lie.

Lotuses scoff under the stone bridges, so pink
     you wonder if touch draws their blood.
          A lotus is not alone

on its wet saucer—roots always connected
     to another's blooming, another's dying.
          Today you are not connected to anything.

Another man offers to draw your portrait.

    So beautiful, he says. *Are you married?*

        You sit on the concrete as he touches a spot

of graphite, forming eyes, a nose, a mouth

    you can't recognize. *Is this beauty?* you wonder.

        Beautiful, this absence, abscess, of love?

Winter Worm, Summer Grass

Now that I   you, wormgrass is on my mind again / Cordyceps—like Cyclops, a one-eyed demon / Sprouting from larva, dreams of warmer seasons / Its Tibetan name is "winter worm, summer grass" / How the horror of it transforms with metaphor / Mind-controlling mold grows on orchids and wet bark / Ghost moth caterpillar, meet demonic fungus / *Hello   how   are you   can we be friends* / Is this meeting an "infection" or a "possession"

A precious parasite feasts on the naïve caterpillar's brains
In girlhood I picked mushrooms and wolfberries from shrubs

and no one warned me about the dangers
just like no one warned me where hope would lead me

down dark hotel corridors filled with dirty dishes and mold spores
Most times   hope is a ghost   it requires exorcism

The way I feel: a pricked thumb bloom / Migratory corpses—the hungry ghosts never satisfied / Eating the wax off burning candles in paper boats / Offerings the townspeople launched gently into the river / Again I let them float like fever down that gully / In Las Vegas I watched your favorite movie, *Farewell My Concubine* / In the bathtub with suds on my face / I was a one-woman Peking Opera troupe / When I got to the part where Leslie Cheung dies, / I wanted to cry but didn't, my ducts were done / Then I watched *A Chinese Ghost Story* and again, Leslie / Falls in love with an abject female ghost / Her sleeves all white and flowing, she died young / And her life was wasted, you see, her beauty unsullied / You told me that once you attended a party at the Mandarin Oriental in Hong Kong / And someone tried to show you the window / Where Leslie jumped

Farmers in Tibet harvest the corpses of the fungal zombie
caterpillars and ship them to every apothecary in Hong Kong,
selling them for $63,000 per pound

Then one cusp of spring you came and visited—it was dank in Manhattan—I lugged your suitcases down the elevator—when we came home, you told me about the stone you were carrying—I wanted to clasp your hand and hold this stone too—we took a cab at 2AM to Lincoln Center—you dreamt of dancing there, when you went to study ballet in Paris as a teenager—together we gawked at the poster of Misty Copeland taller than us—then we snuck into the law school campus at Fordham—on the fourth floor, we danced to "Love on Top"—made the video smiling through our masks—I twirled around you in the empty hallway and you made a heart with your arms—you told me you couldn't meet me where I was—but where was I—on the windy twin peaks in San Francisco—my hands, uprooted like California poppies—on my bed in West Harlem not sleeping, crying—listening to a Faye Wong song "Red Bean"—something about shivering next to each other, how that feels like tenderness, though we've never held hands—the way we walked down Broadway as we approached the Lincoln Center fountain—the way we wandered the Shanghai Bund the first nights we met, years ago—how we walked next to the Huangpu, now the Hudson—everything I wanted to say to you—I said my feelings I wanted to tie to balloons and release into nowhere—the ether—the rivers—like that tinselly red balloon we spotted, stranded and deflating against the corner of the ceiling, in the Rose Main Reading Room at the New York Public Library—somehow it touched the gilded rosettes, scraped the paintings of flaming skies—the day I took you to the places most precious to me—Riverside Park where we walked after putting your laundry in the dryer—I tie this feeling to a balloon, to this poem—when I release it—where will it go—
where will it go

How is it that two fistfuls of these husks
are worth more than my life

The most expensive parasite on earth—
that is a metaphor for love.

Nucleation

The harvesting of pearls, the very process, is a continuous systematic violation of flesh: *insert the mantle tissue of a foreign creature into the oyster shell and wait for its insides to react.* This is called nucleation. Mastication of a foreign object: panicked, the oyster produces nacre. Trapped in the nacre, the invasive agent—the parasite or mantle tissue—is subsumed by the pearl.

To domesticate, then, is to force-feed. Mikimoto, in his dreams, wanted a string of pearls to glow around the neck of every woman in the world. Like the bioluminescent waters of his youth, a deep-sea dive, the pearls became warm upon touch, upon being worn.

Women wear the trauma of other creatures around their necks, in an attempt to put a pall on their own. Adorn the self to be adored. What if we fail? What if we are failures at love? A man once called me "adorable" on a date at a museum. It was hailing outside, and we were wandering through the Death and Transcendence wing. I looked into a woman's tomb, its mother-of-pearl inlays. A limp body looked back, into the gap around my neck. I had no amulet.

Red Tide

The winter that the oysters died,
what was left of their shells
made a leaf in my hand.

        I could see the veins
               where life stopped,

but to my astonishment,
        there were tiny vessels
             that led, still, to the sea.

I thought: what more is possible
inside a catastrophe—wreckage,
wrack of flesh and blood tide—

        creatures married
             to their beds, unable
        to survive? If they won't,

how will I? Toxic algae
blooms, fevering the water
like a poppy field, and I,

        I was ready to give up, hurl
myself into the widowed waves,
        until I stopped to mine

        the deeper oyster
beds, probed the sources
I'd forgotten—
        one, three, five pearls
             rolled onto my palm
against the Fata Morgana, the eventide.

My pink seeds, my darlings!
     Made
              during a massacre,
too precious to plant
     on so doomed an earth,

too stubborn to sleep forever in darkness.

On Shards

reduced to a vessel, the remains of this woman, you

                        smiling in the living organ

        of your little failures

                                    you sent an offering

to the porcelain goddesses: Nüwa, Chang'e, Kuan Yin,

               the Queen Mother of the West

               flipped a coin into the fountain

                       made the wishes

     who can lead a broken life and laugh

                         a bowl's shards silvers / sliver mouth

a temple, a priestess and her crows at sundown

                       the ghosts crying out

never having reached completion

                washing minerals, steeping leeks

                  warm stone under the tongue

the tiny piece of glass inside   your wandering foot

              how a stranger washed it in the empty temple

                  your wandering wound

              and it felt intimate, this stanching, how he cupped the blood

    in his palms

                  bewilderment meant: be wilder

The last Empress of France, the wife of Napoleon
the Third, opened her Chinese Salon in 1863
in the Château de Fontainebleau,
home / Of every French regent
their troves / Their treasures—
Consider when museums
and private collections *acquire*
their objects / How language, like history,

neuters, neutralizes / *Looty*, a dog / *Acquires*, a word
forged in amnesia, shrouding provenance / How the news said
the cop *knelt on* a man's neck / As if the murderer was saying a little
prayer / How protestors *looted* when stocking supplies / "When looting

starts, the shooting starts," the then-president wrote / As rebellion broke
out / The smoke of rubber bullets in their wake / They call this looting
a disgrace / But the smoke of the burnt police station / Remembers

the smoke of the burnt schools / Remembers the smoke
of the bombed-out churches / Remembers the smoke
from rage forged in fire / In Birmingham

In Ferguson / In Tulsa / In Minneapolis
In Louisville / Protestors took off the
right hand of the King Louis XVI statue

How porcelain never tires / Of burning
Smoke from Jingdezhen kilns / Forges
Our chimera / n. *A thing hoped for but in fact*

is impossible / She awakens / In June 2014, I walked
the length of King Louis XVI's château / Left my fingerprints
on his gilt / Found her / My cloisonné enamel chimera / Inside a vitrine

That held my century of humiliation / My looted histories / Then a year
later, in the low light / Before daybreak / A team of thieves would break
into the palace's southwest wing / Purloin the chimera / Steal her back

The Chinese invented porcelain / Ming blue
and white enamels / Persian cobalt oxides
West Lake scenes / yes, the Chinese
have survived centuries
in America, exploited,
excluded, beaten black
and blue / Like their Ming
vases / In an epoch of shame,
war, revolt, famine, and genocide / Yet

this moment / For the allegiance to capital
Or the love of myth / Or the fear of an illusion
My Chinese family / Has forgotten the struggle

They preach law and order / They decry protestors
They defend the blue uniform / They forget what it
Means / To rail for justice/ Maybe they have never
Known / They do not know how it feels like

To mourn a son / They do not want to imagine
They do not dare / They've grown brittle as earthenware
So I am bereft & blue / When I ask *what if it was your son,*
They kick me out / To Angela Davis, Grace Lee Boggs said

We have colonized material, we have colonized people,
we have colonized the earth / The material we've molded
into our possession—kaolin, feldspar, wrangled from earth
A Confucian tradition / To remain insular / To keep fire

Sealed inside imperial kilns / To quiet each rebellion
But every day in America / I want to fight / Baring
A rage my family rejects / Cast me out / I do not
belong / After a long survival, the immigrant

impulse / Is to forget / Vulnerability
Dismiss the struggle for liberation
Cut ties / But nothing, not even
Porcelain, is shatterproof

Heist

On an August day, from Gare de Lyon
we ride the train to the Château de Fontainebleau
to look at looted treasures. When asked

which way to the Chinese Museum,
the guard says: *That section is closed.*
A whole wing sealed off, not a glimpse

afforded for scholars or poets. He leans forward,
whispers, *Have you heard about what happened?*
One year ago, another heist. *The Chinese want*

their treasures back. The French disagree.
This moment, I crave the exhilaration of trespass—
motion sensors, infrared lights to waylay as I walk

across the garden where roses snake around stones,
their heads bent, a punishment for beauty.
In the Empress's chambers where Joséphine,

Eugénie, and Marie Antoinette all lived, walls froth
with pheasants and cornucopias, every corner gilded:
caryatids licking fat grapes, silk drapes from Lyon,

a balustrade from the days of Empire,
all eyesores. Adored, adorned, scorned as
Napoleon's mistresses, the coy subjects of oil

paintings peek from ermine stoles, swollen pearls.
At the exit, we slide into the photo booth
for vintage-style portraits. Travel all this way

in vain—might as well pay a machine ten euros
to look like a dead movie star. Summer: pilfered
light dapples the edges of a stranger's face.

How dear—how dare
we dream like this! That the thing we once
wasted our ardor on, gone in the cloak

of night, would return to us in spring,
unscathed and still alive.

Paris Syndrome

June was a parade of Chinese brides,
       their trains spilling into the gardens.
Blooming gloom, purple sepals—

sweat crowned their frowns, wet diadems
       of dread. Hems, rough hedges—their heads
groomed doll-like for their grooms to glower at.

𤭖

June smelled like perfume
       and piss. Chewing stale bread
on the bridges, I tossed my misgivings
       into the river. How I loved the marble

women in the Tuileries, their inconsolable
weight. To be a monument, stone-carved,
to sorrow. I wandered in search of my own pulse
       between the Monet panels
       in l'Orangerie.

In an airless apartment room on the Rue Eugène
       in the sixteenth arrondissement,
I wrote letters never sent
       to friends long gone. The paper dead
weight in my suitcase. I didn't talk to anyone.

Disconsolation prize: a meal, wet innards,
       a patisserie of one heart pickled
       in many jars.

𤭖

The inability to access the joy you stored in a safe
            to open when the time comes,

when you're somewhere else.
            The joy you hoped
            for in a beautiful country.

Before you could go, you imagined it.
            The possibilities. Wet cornices.
            Plump roasts. A whole other elsewhere
            or romance.

꽃

To burn is to burnish a dead kingdom
            with fine lighting.
Lightning in the sky each night,
            clawing out the sordid eyes
that watch and watch you as you sleep
            in an apartment across from the cemetery
that houses Oscar Wilde's grave.

꽃

I don't know how my mother pictured it. A frame
            for her bones. A house big enough to contain

the past. But no, she never found one.
            The studio we rented

so I could go to school in that district.
            And that makes two regrets.

Before we arrived in the beautiful
         country, I imagined a house
         with walls made of silk.

I imagined a stranger could come up to our door
         and whisper a secret through its seams.

On Silk

In her garden, Empress Leizu watched the fat white worm
feasting on the mulberry leaves,
its mouth a gutter,

a hole, a maw so consumed by consumption
it falls through a hole it has eaten

into her teacup, and once steeped in that bitterness,
the silkworm unravels, retching spools and spools
of thread soft as magnolia, fragrant too,

and the Empress remembered a childhood hunger
so great it turned red like the mulberries

in summer between her fingers, how she picked them
in the woods one day, how her hunger turned her spit red

as she was sated, so she rescued the worm from drowning
and ordered a grove for its endless feast,

and that night all she dreamt of was harvest,
a grove for the mulberry trees,
a loom for the threads to fuse, refuse,

a vat of dye for the white to soak in,
a factory full of girls, as this was women's work,

she knew something beautiful as silk required sacrifice,
so she planted the seed, pulped the pupa, reaped the dream—

a garden full of maiden silkworms
growing fat but never growing.

꽃

In Chang'an, the emperor wanted
to expel the nomads from the margins.
His weapon: warhorses—"heavenly horses"
from the desert. Parasites drank
from their muscles, so these horses
leaked red sweat. The blood on the silk
was theirs, spilled where the silk road began.

꽃

                    In my travels, I wore thrifted silk dresses.
                    The material grew damp with fishy sweat.
                    I wondered about the previous wearers, where
                    they went and what they did. I gave my dresses
                    to my poet friends. Jane wore my green silk
                    dress gathering mussels in a tidepool. In my
                    dream, the silk jacket from my childhood tore
                    against the branches in the high winds,
                    then floated, skeletal, like a body in a river—

꽃

Nomads love silk. For lifetimes
they've walked the desert. The light material
exposed their skin to the kisses of a long
cool breeze. Easy resistance
to mirage.

꽃

                    Years ago, I visited Suzhou, world capital
                    of silk and wedding dresses. At the Silk Museum,
                    the silkworms crumpled themselves in baskets,

lazy and dazed in the spoils of mulberry.

       weft / weave / reeling / warp / dye

After the first molting, the second molting,
silk moths lay eggs. Then the weavers—at the
museum, these wax dolls—brought offerings
to the gods of sericulture.

𧶠

Before currency, before mint or coin,
there were bolts of silk
spun by women and *Bombyx mori*.
The loom, the threads, the hands, the cocoons,
the moon looming over the singing dunes. The moon eating
crape myrtle and organza.

𧶠

On Guanqian Street, the shops lined up
next to the canals—the Lingering Garden,
the Lions Grove Garden, where drunk poets
recited poems to amber carp eating dead
skin off their feet. That year, I was trying
to reconstruct myself with a thin,
lightweight, breathable material. I bought
a silk qipao patterned with moonflowers,
wondered where on earth I could wear it.

𧶠

The Romans coveted silk, for it clung
to the body, left nothing
to imagine, scandalizing men.
Japan sent an envoy to steal cocoons
and kidnap two young silk-weavers

holding the secret of sericulture.
At night the two women looked
at the moon, tried to divulge the secret,
revealed not by tongue but hands,
which were roped to their backs
in case they attempted escape.

ꠥ

Life is a magnificent gown infested with fleas.
—EILEEN CHANG

Shanghai, 2018: I wore the qipao to the Eileen
Chang-themed café in the Jing'an District, in
Eileen's former residence, Changde Apartment.
She lived there in the 1940s, wrote *Romances* and
Love in a Fallen City. My friend, visiting from
Kunming, said Eileen's advice for wearing qipao
is not to be afraid of showing off the belly's
curve. I imagine Eileen lounging on her sixth-
floor balcony, her qipao taut across her belly.
Once, a man slipped a note under her door, and
in that apartment their romance began. In that
apartment, their affair also ended. She moved out
soon after. Life begins as a worm spinning spools
of spit-cocoon, ends as a flea-infested gown.
Embroidered in golden thread, a bouquet of
lilies—daily, in the same narrow room, the
sunlight begins, and always ends.

ꠥ

red coral, topaz, lapis lazuli / religion, contagion / spices, agate, copper

red sea pearls, apricots, jade / glassware, silver, indigo / frankincense

peaches from Samarkand / spider silks, wild silks / raw at every edge

卍

> I wore the qipao to the Fairmont Peace Hotel,
> the first floor, a club where the Old Jazz Band
> played every night. My friend from New York
> was visiting—she wore my qipao, the one I
> found in Hangzhou, bright and turquoise with
> red orchids. We watched a lovely woman
>
> dance in front of the band—she smiled
> in her white dress, her arms wildly swinging.
> *Would you believe it? I am sixty-five,*
> she said, waiting for us to say, *No! We don't*
> *believe you! How can you laugh and dance like*
> *that, having lived for all these years?*

卍

rose agate / cinnabar, high winds / mouth of a golden snake / minarets, musks, and melons

卍

> Everywhere in Shanghai, I saw the painted
> Shanghai ladies. In 1930s advertisements, they
> smiled compulsively, dressed in qipao and furs, as
> if they weren't living through a civil war, an
> occupation, the threat of war, an invasion.

Everything crackling, everything burning, but
these glamorous women kept smiling in these
paintings, even after time ran out, their smiles so
charming they sell osmanthus perfume oil,
which I bought at a cosmetics shop in Yuyuan
Garden, and wear on my neck to this very day.

卍

At the mouth of the Silk Road,
in the desert outside Dunhuang,
a rumor of voices slurring in the sand.

Among the eroded land formations,
parched for silk and unspoiled girls,
cosmologies, maladies and gods,
merchants traveling all night, shelter.

What did the wanderer hear on her way
to a deathless house? West —an entryway.
Not a mirage but a ghost shrieking for water—

卍

But real Shanghai ladies were melancholy. Ruan
Lingyu, the actress who died of melancholia at
24. Zhou Xuan, the golden voice of the Seven
Singing Stars of Shanghai, whose fame propelled
the hit song "The Wandering Songstress," died
in a Shanghai mental asylum at 37.

卍

Unspooling a bolt of raw silk, a wandering
songstress lays across the threads, prays to Canmu,
Mother of Silkworms, before vanishing in the sand,
no longer prey to the desert's vagaries.

꿔

The first floor of the Fairmont Peace Hotel,
there is a hall full of trompe l'oeil storefronts
from the 30s. A silk shop, a shoe shop, a qipao
on display. These days, ordinary women posed
for photoshoots in red silk gowns, downstairs at
the entrance to the hotel—I recall the Langston
Hughes poem "Red Silk Stockings"—

꿔

When I first arrived in the desert, I desperately
wanted to be the first female explorer to cross
the Sahara.
    —SANMAO, "A KNIFE ON A DESERT NIGHT"

꿔

1934: Langston Hughes visited Shanghai,
when the Fairmont Peace Hotel went by
another name, the Cathay. He wrote: *I was*
more afraid of going into the world-famous
Cathay Hotel than I was of going into any public
place in the Chinese quarters. Colored people
are not welcomed at the Cathay.

At the exclusive clubs on the Bund, no Chinese
were allowed. According to Hughes: *I was*
constantly amazed in Shanghai at the impudence

of white foreigners in drawing a color line
against the Chinese in China itself.

श्री

When I found the water, I debated
drinking its mirage. In the desert,
everything grew wild. I expected
an expanse of death, but everything
sprouted before me, more alive
than I could ever hope to be.

श्री

Every evening in the Bund, orange light
bathed the municipal buildings as I strolled.
The cameras captured every transgression—
jaywalking or loitering. On this side of the river,
memories of blood spilled. A luxury watch brand
sells time to the rivers of people walking down
East Nanjing Road.

They'd waited a lifetime to witness this skyline
across the Huangpu River. Pudong, sequined
with fishscale lights, projections on buildings—
cherry blossoms, ads for skin cream, and the
words *I love my home*, in Chinese and English.
Junks rimmed with briny lights. Even the sky
was a bolt of silk torn in half by God.

How the splendor and squalor of our collective
past could transform overnight. A worm spitting
and spinning itself into a new luxury, a sensation,
finally, yes, a thing of value.

Nature Morte

Dead nature or still life, let me be still and alive
for a moment on this table with the mutant persimmon,

the comb with missing teeth, and seven white hairs
from my scalp. The Henri Charles Guérard etching

Les cocottes de la mort pairs five pieces of origami
with a human skull. If you stare hard into the sockets

of that skull, you may see the hibernating animal.
It breathes faintly. The heart in its ribs knows it is hunted

not for medicine but profit. For greed. This season ahead,
I will try to hibernate. I will draw the same portrait

of a dead woman in graphite, gouache, ink. November,
I line her brows. December, I color her ears. I attempt

chiaroscuro to make her surfaces appear three-dimensional.
At many points in life, you will lose your will to keep

going. Outside the studio, the kingdom falls. The ice
sheets migrate. Another planet, they plead. Another social

order, I plead. In the dappled darkness, I sip burnt coffee.
Degraded, the soil goes from soft to fibrous. Degraded,

the water stops irrigating its land. Degraded, the reef turns
white with fear—it ghosts the seafloor. It halts. Degraded,

a woman is still a woman. She might turn red, burn a bit.
She's already an undesirable color. I try to correct. I paint

over her face before she suffers more. Now the portrait
is a still life. All we see of her form are her hands reaching

toward the basket of bruised pears. All they seek is fruit.
All they find is a skull, the bit of hardened bread.

On Majolica

Queen Victoria loved her pugs.
Spitz and spaniel couldn't compare—
the Chinese dogs were imported,

bred breathless and wheezing,
snorting with terror-struck bells
for eyes. No wonder why so many

were shaped, painted, and baked
in a kiln, reproduced by Minton & Co.,
inventor of majolica, that soft-bodied

ceramic. Whatever the Queen loved,
the public loved too. She had other
pets, to be sure—an African grey

parrot, a Shetland pony, a Persian goat,
all servile creatures she coddled
and punished. Victorian England

settled on imperial obsessions. Majolica
garden seat, shape no. 589: a monkey
holds a cushion up, inviting its owner

to sit. A three-dimensional trompe l'oeil,
a nod to Darwin's theories. To conquer
is to popularize the image—and testify

that an animal begs for its own conquest.
The trouble with tropics and so much frond
is that the sun bronzes skin and breeds the basest

urges, according to the denizens of temperate
climes, whose lives were neutered by civility
and the Crown. Nevertheless, a craze emerged

for those trinkets, mad rush to buy ceramic
marmosets, soft-bodied pugs. "Exotic" always sold
out fastest. "Civil" households couldn't get enough.

🦎

London's Great Crystal Palace Exhibition, 1851:
        in Prince Albert's palace of glass and iron,
Minton debuted his invention, majolica, named

        it after the tin-glazed wares of Palissy,
in a fountain of sumptuous color—leaden with gloss
        and scarred lung, coughs. Optical illusion
ravishing—the audience oohed, aahed, captive

        like the rajah's stuffed elephant
decked in pearls. Wonder is the sum of spoils.
        All this awe, a reliquary, unable to contain
                its human blood.

🦎

The Great London International Exhibition of 1862
                showcased treasures, loot
from the sacking of the Old Summer Palace. Lord
                Elgin, High Commissioner

of the Opium War, ordered its arson, then distributed
                a sale catalogue of bronzes, jade,
cloisonné porcelains ripped from the Gardens of Ease,
                named for an extinction.

汉

The Aesthetic Movement began in the 1860s,
                as "a return to natural beauty"
inspired by Asian arts and wares. But "inspiration"
                is the wrong word for a forced opening,

how the US military forced Japan to open its borders,
                how Britain force-fed opium to China,
so the pretty wares of Aestheticism could enchant
                regular British households—plum branches, sprigs
                of holly and ivy, fans and lacquerware,

British imitations of Chinese-style jardinieres
                with paw feet, of wilted chrysanthemum vases
                and psychedelic dragon teapots, their lopsided
claws catching, spilling blue-and-white waves.

汉

The glassy-colored glazes were leaden
and heavy metal, as paintresses

in the factories rouged the cherub's

cheeks, swabbed the stork's eye,
froze each palm leaf into its stencil—

how the paintress sniffed the lead, snuffed

out the flaws, and all the bright young ladies
grew dull and dim, tossed their lives

to avoid getting fired, and when the lead-

paint glazes were fired in the kiln
for that signature shine, the majolica wares

emerged, benign again, non-toxic

to the lips of their buyers. The rich man
slurped a real Chesapeake oyster

from its decoy twin, carved in pink,

as the girl who painted its vulnerable
blush died in her sleep of lead poisoning

before she tasted the figs she colored,

before she mastered the mixture.
A thousand oysters she painted, in a lifetime,

but never once touched one with her lips.

Poppies and Jade

In the Peacock Room of the Freer Gallery of Art, the blue-and-white porcelain jardiniere floats on a velvet bed. Forged in the Qing dynasty, the jardiniere is symmetrical. So many have died for a symmetry like this.

The color, too. A blue-white line divides the reverie from the suffering life. So many poisoned—blue so deep its cut would clean a gash or sharpen the edges of a dream. Or a red cadmium satin glaze so hot it butters the bisque in fever. Carmine—like poppies, their crepe pistils dusting the edges of a mouth.

Would you rather: a pistil or a pistol?

罌

Poppy harvests in the spring. Soporific, silk crepe over eyelids. Crown and sepal, a stigma, a strain. A poppy bloom in dung. To extract the drug, dig into the whorl inside the flower. Poppy tea, poppy seeds. The spice trade also a poppy trade—a process: to plant, implant, extract.

罌

In the next hall: jade. Finials, dials, little carved dogs with tongues hanging out. The late pharmaceutical giant Arthur M. Sackler imparted his name to this gallery and donated from his renowned Chinese collection—

1) a finial in the form of a human hybrid (jade)
2) an ornament in the shape of a mask (jade)
3) a pendant in the form of a bird with horns
4) ancestor tablets, flanged bracelets
5) a set of ancient bronze bells without tongues

罌

Dame Jillian Sackler has been trying to clear her late husband's name. In his lifetime, Arthur M. Sackler made his fortune selling valium and deploying marketing strategies later adopted by his relatives to peddle OxyContin.

Decades ago, at an antique store, Arthur Sackler fell in love with a Chinese rosewood table, launching his expensive obsession. What did he see in the red-brown timber of that table? Its rough finish, its deep veins? Its curved carvings, propelling a lifetime's worth of violent cravings?

In a thrift shop on West 78th Street, I saw a kelly-green Chinese armoire tied in the back with a tag that said, "Best of—to be displayed." An older European man loved it so much he asked the manager if he could pay in cash. "Money is no issue," he said. "I just want to buy it."

敭

European and American Chinamania began in the nineteenth century. Chinamania coincided with the Opium Wars in Europe and in America, the mass murders of Chinese laborers and the passage of the Chinese exclusion laws.

With Chinamania, Western households went wild for Chinese-style tea sets, vases, fans, silk shawls, furniture, ewers, spoons, and others. From palaces to parlors, from rich to middle-class the porcelain spread, a commodity likened to a disease. It was the origins of mass consumer culture. Meanwhile, the Chinese men who built the railroads in America drowned in mud banks and their bodies were dumped into the canals.

Museums and palaces in Europe displayed classical Chinese objects and harbored illustrious collections—the Rijksmuseum, the Château de Fontainebleau, the Victoria and Albert Museum, the British Museum, etc.

敭

I examined the armoire closer. Carved into its brass center was a poem. On Wechat I asked my dad what the words meant. A famous Tang poem, he told me. The imperfect computer-generated translation:

Ruthless is the Taicheng willow / Nanjing,
ancient capital, has vanished like a dream / Floating in an embankment.

泥

Sackler soon amassed a priceless collection of jades and bronzes. Nephrite and jadeite, the hardest stones. A set of bronze bells without tongues, without clappers, which meant that to produce a sound, one had to use a mallet from the outside. The ancient bells now sit at the gallery, never to clang. The Sackler name is now notorious. A synonym for pain, after they claimed to have found its cure inside the fortune inside the opium poppy inside the jade hairpin of a dead queen inside the ransacked tomb inside Lord Elgin's order to annihilate.

泥

In 2021, the Metropolitan Museum of Art announced it was removing the name Sackler from the Sackler Wing. That wing houses the Temple of Dendur, a tomb carved from Aeolian sandstone. It also houses four ancient statues of the Goddess Sekhmet, the goddess of force, rebirth, and ethereal destruction.

When I visited, a private event was underway. Flasks, glasses, champagne, centerpieces all set out for absent mystery guests. No one could enter the temple or shiver in its sanctuary. The white tablecloths far away, ten feet from the wrath of the goddesses.

泥

At panels, luncheons, and speaking engagements, men tell me that their wives and girlfriends are Chinese or Taiwanese or from Hong Kong. Sometimes they whisper it while looking at me. I wonder if they hear themselves as echoes.

At a Beijing foreign correspondents' party, a white man grabbed my ass as I exited and when I turned around, he spewed, *I thought you were my wife. I mistook you for my wife!* Later, a petite Asian woman apologized and bowed to me on behalf of her husband, but I noticed that I looked nothing like her. She was wearing black and white. In red, I was a whole head taller.

猿

I imagined the man bringing the armoire home to place next to his other chinoiserie. Perhaps I was being unfair—protective of something not mine. But the words inscribed in that chest were the words inscribed in mine. In my rental apartment still unfurnished, there was nowhere to put this chest, and anyway, I didn't have the strength to haul it. I imagined the armoire built from the bones of a willow tree or a rosewood. Once, it was carefree, no poems weighing heavy in its heart. Floating in an embankment, the willow's hair long, drinking from the jade gourd. Weeks later, I waited in line and finally bought it.

猿

From the Sackler Gallery's staircase, you can view the sculpture *Monkey Grasps at the Moon*, a 2001 commissioned piece by the artist Xu Bing. The sculpture suspends the word Monkey in twenty-one languages, each ideograph like a vertebra on a spine.

The tale goes: Long ago, a group of monkeys wanted so badly to touch the pale full moon. So they linked arms, reaching down from a peach tree to touch her. But when they descended, all they touched was water. On a full night, the moon towered, reflecting the monkey's heart, a chimera.

Down on the first floor, I see the water, no moon, but a handful of pennies and nickels. Chimeras, coins. I wonder if any of these wishes have come true.

猿

Risking fall, a monkey grasps at the moon.
A reflection, mere mirror, of her magnificent beauty.
Was the moon an impotent love? Was it unattainable?
Languages tangle on the tongue, linking arms, as if attempting
communication. Why bother?
Monkey, monkey on his journey to the west, eats
a peach of immortality and plucks poppies, drawing blood.
Blood in the water feeds the carp.
Along the embankment, willows veil a nephrite moon.
Monkeys kiss the moon and then their insides harden,
vitrify. Cold, petrified stone. The jade rabbit
in my wooden chest eats the dust.

The Queen's Room

*—San Francisco auction block where the first
immigrant Chinese women were sold as sex slaves*

Note the tasteful draperies over the windows,
the view of the canneries. Salt air-gagged, we
arrived west. Sunburnt necks. Teenagers, most of us.
Like tanagers. Over the sea, we were red-winged,
ready. The men who made us come here feigned
betrothal. Had us on our backs and talked of gold.
Now so many pretty girls lewd and unaccompanied.
Debarking the ship, we were led to the barracoons.
The bidders waited. Why call it a Queen's room?
A hundred and fifty jewels clothed in lice and rags
up for the highest bidder. Our mouths, cash cows
for our "husbands." Forced to sign contracts we
could not read, we did not know the words,
did not know *merchant* or *earthquake* or *gold*,
did not know *debt* or *price* or *penny* or *worth*.

Aubade with Gravel and Gold

I'm sick of speaking for women who've died
Their stories and their disappearances
bludgeon me in my sleep

Their language is the skein in my throat
that unravels every time a bullhorn blows,
every time a road

is paved, every time a railroad
is constructed, ballast to blast, built to last

against the orange flames
of an open, unwritten sky

The bad ballad
of a silenced, hell–bent woman
bled its way into my jaws

And I wake up this morning, every morning
eating my disquiet

Crack my window open, their breath rushes in
Me, this body, the same weight
of disappearance, same weight
of fortune

Last night a woman from another century
entered me, and her male phantoms possessed
me, all night I was warm,
cold and savage with their touch

Heatless factories shorn of silk, muslin,
and selvage, machineries like guns,

no salve for the women's cracked hands,
no salvaging their rations, their ambitions
for survival

There was the child of a famine
There was a girl sold for three gilded ounces
at the old San Francisco port

They sailed, they sailed, they sailed through me
and I turned gold with that touch

One Thousand Boats

Yayoi Kusama, Gertrude Stein Gallery, New York, 1963

Summer 2013: at the Stedelijk Museum, the boat
      overflows with handmade penises.
In 1963, the artist sewed thousands of these

      despite her abject fear of dick. Revulsion
transforms into a burial, a ritual of obliteration.
      In her autobiography, Kusama wrote,

It was only by doing this that I gradually turned
      the horror into something familiar.
Imagine having a penis phobia, then stitching

      a thousand phalluses together, gluing
them to the hull of a ship. Imagine the nightmares:
      a choppy sea, a monster gust, icy rain

and tumbling oars, a bed of black mambas
      swarming the only lifeboat in sight.
I imagine rowing that boat to a place far away

      from any flesh and blood I know—
far away, the world bursts into infinite colors—
      wisteria, gunpowder, smells long

extinct returning to the senses like phantoms.
      Sail through this fear, beyond its dirty haze!
Every penis is a liminal space. I surrender—

      cure my bloodlust, cure my penis envy,
my phallic frenzy, with the spell of red flowers
      and a dragnet for fools. I venture

into the orgiastic summer, and though my fear
        is never cured, I dream harder, adventure
deeper. Obliterate: turn your everyday horrors

        into what's familiar. Obliterate doom,
obliterate time, obliterate enemies. Go where
        you don't recognize the flora or fauna.

In a dazzled forest, regale yourself with your fears.

The Kingdom of Surfaces

Looking-Glass House

> *In Lewis Carroll's* Through the Looking-Glass, and What Alice Found There *(1871),*
> *the heroine enters an imaginary, alternative universe by climbing through a mirror in her*
> *house. In this world, a reflected version of her home, everything is topsy-turvy and back-to-*
> *front. Like Alice's make-believe world, the China mirrored in the fashions in this exhibition*
> *is a fictional, fabulous invention, offering an alternate reality with a dreamlike illogic.*

On a spring afternoon in 2015, I emerge from the 77th Street station on Lexington Street, on my way to a newly opened exhibition at the Met, *China: Through the Looking Glass*. The main entrance of the Metropolitan Museum of Art is a threshold into a mythopoeia, decked in fragments, petroglyphs of feathers. It's cool and inviting, there is another air, another scent, nothing like the wet hum and bruised leaves of outside.

Andrew Bolton, the curator, names his introduction of the exhibition "Toward an Aesthetic of Surfaces." Alluding to Barthes, Voltaire, Swift, it's a love letter to artifice. A love letter to pastiche. Are the surfaces of these fantasies fragile, are they strong enough to break my fingers? I peer into the displays. The glass vitrines hold cinnabar screens, porcelain, cloisonné enamel bowls from lustrous dynasties. Motionless amid these things, dresses by John Galliano bedeck mannequins. Silks and sequins, sumptuous textures, embroideries—all otherworldly like fish scales stolen from the bodies of real creatures.

I am searching for the Looking-Glass house, a portal. The surface doesn't dissolve magically to the touch. This surface is a mirror, a seam. I am in love with it the way I am afraid to love another human. To love a pretty object that is not allowed to be touched. To love a pretty object as time colludes with its disappearance. To disappear into enchantment.

Do these surfaces awe me? *Yes.* My own yes disturbs me.

The Garden of Live Flowers

Stylistically, they belong to the practice of Orientalism, which since the publication of Edward Said's seminal treatise on the subject in 1978 has taken on negative connotations of Western supremacy and segregation. At its core, Said interprets Orientalism as a Eurocentric worldview that essentializes Eastern peoples and cultures as a monolithic other.

In Lewis Carroll's tome, glass is not a border—in fact, it becomes immaterial, a silvery mist you can breathe in. Opacity has a way of tricking us into believing something is impenetrable. Glass becomes gauze becomes haze, and in that haze, the little girl enters the mirror.

Wandering through the halls, I forget who I am and what I'm wearing—a blue cornflower dress with an empire waist, stitched in a silk factory in China, by the hands of a young woman.

There are no wild silkworms left in the world. For humans to harvest silk, the silkworm has to die. Cocoons thrown in boiling water. If the silkworm survives and becomes a silk moth, the silk is ruined. Everything beautiful contains in its kernel a suggestion of suffering, of death. Otherwise, it would just be pretty and uncomplicated.

In the hallway, a voice calls out, *I've been waiting for you.* I follow the voice past the crepe evening gowns, past the hall of mirrors, into a bright phantasmagoria. Wisteria surrounds a willow tree, a pagoda, and three bridges, all painted Ming blue. The voice belongs to the willow. All around its branches, the wisteria whispers. The décor comes alive. Is it geomancy? Their breath makes me wistful. I choke.

A sign points to the next room. The main early Buddhist sculpture hall displays what they call a Bamboo Garden. The Chinese name of the exhibition is "Mirror Flower Water Moon." A fiber-optic kingdom, mimicking the moonrise over a lake. A thousand plexiglass rods emit LED lights, and their silvery forms move like snakes or anemones or Medusa's hair. If you tie a snake into a knot and cinch it, its spine breaks and it goes into shock. But if it's a loose knot, the snake bends without breaking.

The bamboo LED forest snakes around the Buddhist sculptures, trapping the mannequins inside. The mannequins wear pretty hats designed by a famous milliner from London. One mannequin faces a window—could that be the Looking-Glass House? The lattice peers into a garden of infernal flora. The flowers of perdition, all red. Opium poppies, the landscape I can't quite make out. I touch it and a hole opens on its surface. It's turning into mist. I vanish.

Looking-Glass Insects

While neither discounting nor discrediting the issue of representation of "subordinated otherness" outlined by Said, this exhibition attempts to propose a less politicized and more positivistic examination of Orientalism as a site of infinite and unbridled creativity.

I emerge through the gilded mist, and a door appears. Instead of the hellscape I imagined, the door opens to another exhibition, a sunken version of the same bright museum.

Sweat pearls the nape of my neck—the LED lights have gone dark, the music silenced. Wisteria withers in basins of rainwater. The willow moans. Live foxes wander, sniffing each other's tails—red foxes and arctic foxes, hunting slender fawns. It's an absolute wilderness inside this museum, and I am amazed at the aliveness—the teeth, the insects, the flytraps, the jug plants.

Where am I?

You are inside your own pretend game, the blue willow replies.

As I walk onward, the display cases shatter. Objects tumble at my feet. A cigarette box, an urn, a sugar bowl, a vase. I open the box; inside, jewel-bright insects with razor-sharp wings. Proboscises of rare bugs gleaming in jewels. Dazzled, I touch them and disgust myself. I really am a huntress desiring the blood of my sister, the night.

But beauty is political. But beauty is political. But beauty is political.

The woods bloom, and I reach the forest where things have no names. Stranded here, a wounded fawn licks itself. I see myself reflected in its wound.

The blue dress is beginning to melt off as I enter another terrible portal. My body is a projector screen. Someone's fantasy is coming true. Someone is thrilled. Someone is delighted. Someone is loving this. When someone's fantasy comes true, my nightmare begins.

Wool and Water

Through careful juxtapositions of Western fashions and Chinese costumes and decorative arts, it presents a rethinking of Orientalism as an appreciative cultural response by the West to its encounters with the East. The ensuing dialogues are not only mutually enlivening and enlightening, but they also encourage new aesthetic interpretations and broader cultural understandings.

I am trapped in someone else's imagination. My borders lose shape. I become a woman without boundaries, permeable as water. From my mouth, sepals fall. From my skin, armor and scales slough off. I am a silkworm before the harvest. In my throat, a protest—but no sound escapes, except the soporific sound of a reed flute. *Where am I?* I try to ask. *Whose fantasy is this? What are the implications of living in your fantasy?* Nothing. No answers.

In the next hall, there is a party. Is this . . . the Met Gala? The flowers of perdition lavish the museum with a pungent scent. Across the columns, women dressed like empresses get in formation. Rihanna in gold Guo Pei and fox furs, Beyonce in a Givenchy gown, Lupita in sparkling Prada feathers, Fan Bingbing in a peacock green cape—all of these costumes I've seen in pictures. At the end of their procession, the Red Queen walks.

She is wearing a red wool shawl over her gown made of pink opium poppies, and her crown is wrapped around her neck. An aquiline mask shrouds her face. She takes it off, revealing herself as Anna Wintour. *You!* she shouts, pointing at me. *You are not on the guest list!*

There is a seating chart taped to the wall. Scanning the list of guests, I recognize the names of those dead and alive, like some postapocalyptic rendition of The Dinner Party by Judy Chicago. My name isn't there. The ground is a chessboard, and I am not even a pawn. Truman Capote dons a mask from his Black and White Ball. Edna St. Vincent Millay, Anna May Wong, F. Scott Fitzgerald, Frida Kahlo, Sylvia Plath, Andy Warhol, Jean-Michel Basquiat—they turn. André Leon Talley walks toward me with a mic. *Did you eat Chinese food this week?* he asks.

The rest of my dress dissolves into water, falling off of me in rivulets. I search for escape, but the air is thick as liquid. I row with my arms, trying to return to the window I climbed into. The same mannequin I encountered is cowering in a corner, crying. Tears gush down the mannequin's face, but it has no eyes. *Why are you crying?* I ask, but it doesn't have the mouth to answer.

Humpty Dumpty

The China that unfolds before our eyes is a China "through the looking glass," one that is culturally and historically decontextualized. Freed from settings, past and present, the objects in this catalogue and in the exhibition galleries begin to speak for and between themselves. A narrative space opens up that is constantly being reorganized by free associations. Meanings are endlessly negotiated and renegotiated.

Lewis Carroll published *Through the Looking-Glass, and What Alice Found There* in 1871, the same year as the Chinese Massacre in Los Angeles, where nineteen Chinese immigrants were robbed, tortured, and hung by a mob of more than five hundred white men in a single alley in what is now downtown, near Union Station. It was one of the largest mass lynchings in American history.

The 1870s, the height of the Gilded Age, when moguls built monuments out of blood sacrifices. 1871, one decade after the Second Opium War. 1871, two years after the completion of the Transcontinental Railroad. 1871, one decade before the Chinese Exclusion Act. 1871, sixteen years before the Snake River Massacre, which left the bodies of thirty-four Chinese men dead in a dusky Oregon valley called Hells Canyon. In one ranch home, a Chinese skull was fashioned into a decorative sugar bowl.

If you decontextualize the history from the bowl and place it on a kitchen table, what do you have? A varnished object, whose function is to hold sugar. Sugar sweetened the ranch hand's morning coffee, sweetened the whipping cream, the cakes and tarts. The purpose of sugar—pleasure. Sensation. What a treat. Skull, sockets, nineteenth-century cane field. If you place the decorative sugar bowl in a museum exhibition, what do you get? An even brighter elevation! When a curator smiles, he gives us permission to enjoy the sugar bowl for pure aesthetic value.

I am sitting on the ground in someone's fantasy, in the plundered exhibition hall. Naturally I'm naked—my body belongs not to me but to all who behold it. *Imagine doing something to this*, my placard would read. The window portal is solid now. There is no escape. I find myself talking to a lacquered bowl behind a glass display case. It is sitting precariously on a wall—I fear it would fall and crack, but it doesn't believe me. It tells me it's unbreakable.

What makes you so confident? I ask, envying the bowl's assurance.

If I break, the King will come and restore me with his army and his knights. It's all but guaranteed that my rights are protected.

I'm glad you could have such trust in the system.

I'd be a traitor if I didn't, the bowl says. *And you, Missy, where are you from? You don't look like you belong here.*

Tweedledum and Tweedledee

There is a tonic effect in the placement of Western fashions alongside Chinese costumes and decorative arts. Mutually enlivening and mutually enlightening, the resulting visual or aesthetic dialogues encourage new mimetic and referential readings that are based on subjective rather than objective assessments.

I walk away from the bowl that is about to break. Standing in tall grass, I fashion a dress out of weeds and thorns. Two partygoers spot me and shout, *Intruder!*

I recognize them: Chang and Eng Bunker, the Siamese twins, in the flesh! Eng is dashing in his custom-made Armani tuxedo, coattails streaming behind him like pennants. Chang is dashing too in his Qing dynasty robe. I crouch in the corner in my sad weed dress, and Chang, the kind one, hands me a spare robe. They argue with each other, Eng wanting to turn me in, Chang wanting to keep me there.

We'll hide you, they finally say, leading me through an ornate dragon door with a padlock. We enter a set for a music video. The makeup artists seat me and paint my face white with lead. *In this world, we check our souls at the door*, says Chang as they paint him with kohl. *But in exchange for playing along, we make a lot of money*, says Eng as they paint him with yellow.

When we were younger, we used to tour the country as a freak show, says Chang as they rouge his clown lips. *But now we just live off our offspring*, says Eng as they slant his chink eyes.

The music video is "The Princess of China." It's a song by Coldplay. The plot goes like this: Eng and Chang are evil twins who kidnap me from the Forbidden City—a plaster labyrinth complete with apsaras, flying ninjas, and red pagodas—try to auction me off, and fail. They smuggle me across an unknown border and imprison me in their Siamese dungeon. A White Knight played by Chris Martin or Matt Damon or whoever rescues me, kills the twins by stabbing them through the liver that connects them, and in exchange for my freedom, I have to let the White Knight invent me. And because he invents me, he also gets to fuck me. After he fucks me, he leaves me by the side of the road with a bag of moldering apples, salutes *good luck*. I am supposed to enjoy my "freedom," but I can't, because without his imagination, I don't exist.

I cannot speak unless they are lines from this script. In protest, I tear the script into pieces. An earthquake rips the ground—props rattle, chalices quiver, the whole set is falling apart. *You won't escape*, threatens the director. *We'll write you back into this story and you won't survive it this time.*

With that, the twins open the door again, ushering me out. *You must go to the Eighth Square. Once you get to the Eighth Square, you'll become Queen.*

The Lion and the Unicorn

As if by magic, the distance between East and West, spanning perspectives that are often perceived as monolithic and diametrically opposed, diminishes. So, too, does the association of the East with the natural and the authentic and the West with the cultural and the simulacrum.

Dresses from the exhibition float behind glass, alive with beating hearts. The Chinese objects, too, are living—I hear their pulses. Each object has a label: ROMANTIC. ENIGMATIC. MYSTICAL. The throne of the Empress Dowager holds its breath. In front of its display, a Lion and a Unicorn are sparring. The Unicorn bites off a chunk of the Lion's mane. The Lion mauls the Unicorn, scratching its left eye.

Fabulous monster, the Unicorn calls Alice when it first sets its eyes on her in *Through the Looking Glass.* Alice responds *I always thought unicorns were fabulous monsters, too!* Their pact was simple: If you'll believe in me, I'll believe in you. But in the corridor where I stand there looking, all I muster is a purr or a whimper. Against my better judgment, I scramble the other way, toward the dresses. The first dress is a yellow sequined gown by Tom Ford from the 2004–2005 Yves Saint Laurent collection. I remember the qipao tops sold in 2004 for $12.99 a pop at the Westfield Valley Fair mall in San Jose, California. How they embarrassed me: to wear them is to wear a cheap version of your heritage, the source of your shame.

The second piece, a pink silk jacquard coat embroidered with polychrome silk thread, is by John Galliano for House of Dior, autumn/winter 1998–99 Haute Couture collection. Of his inspiration, Galliano says: *Before I visited China, it was the fantasy that drew me to it, the sense of danger and mystery.* The price of incandescence— more than plenitudes of money or blood or desire. Despite my horror, I covet. I covet draping the garments over my eyes, I covet their caress. How silk stretches against skin, a tactile intimacy akin to protection.

The third piece is a dress donated by Anna May Wong herself, a black silk charmeuse gown embroidered with a gold sequin dragon, designed by Travis Banton in 1934. She wore this dress in the film *Limehouse Blues.*

The dresses speak in unison: *Wear me. Wear me. Wear me.* I walk inside the glass vitrine of the dress I choose. Anna May's face peers down at me from its ceiling: a black-and-white image of her raising her arms, her hands over her eyes. As I touch the charmeuse, the dragon stitched into the dress slips out of its seams, roaring into three-dimensionality. It tears the Lion to shreds. It tears the Unicorn to shreds. Oh, my sight burns! It is a thing to behold: the gleaming golden serpent with blood on its teeth. Before I could scream, it brands me with hot pokers—its mouth finds the back of my neck. I try to scream—then fall into a river leading to the main exhibition hall. Pain mushrooms into numbness. The venom turns my skin green, translucent—in the looking glass, I see my own bones through my chest. What is this fabulous monster, barely surfacing? It is me. It is me. It is me.

"It's My Own Invention"

Cinema often serves as a conduit for this reciprocal exchange. Film is frequently the first lens through which Western designers encounter Chinese imagery, and this exhibition explores the impact of movies in shaping their fantasies.

The water doesn't heal me, but my blood seems to make the river stronger. In the current, I swim. I am a human piece of driftwood floating in an intolerable river. It rushes into another hallway of mirrors. Ahead, a woman clothed in a long blue-and-white robe stands on a boat.

It's Anna May Wong, holding an oar. Crowned with a diadem, snow, and a silk cocoon, she is the White Queen. I call out to her. Like the White Queen in Lewis Carroll's story, Anna May's memories run in both directions: the past, when all the cinemas were silent, and the future, when the snows on every mountain melt. She pulls me into her boat and hands me her oar.

Reeling from the serpent bite, my body is covered with blue welts. *These are the same welts suffered by the first Chinese immigrant women in America*, Anna May says. *One generation before I was born, women poured into the ports of San Francisco, and they were sold in slave auctions right on the docks. By day they toiled in factories, by night they toiled with their bodies—if they transgressed, they were branded with hot pokers.*

The White Queen continues: *In order to wreck the dream, you have to infect it from inside its skin.* I can tell she has already lived in this fantasy for so long, smoldered it from the inside out.

The river vanishes suddenly. Now we are on the set of *Limehouse Blues*. In the black charmeuse dress—the one whose serpent bit me—Anna May Wong takes the stage. The audience grunts, cheers. She slips into the Dragon Lady role with strange dignity. The song goes: *In Limehouse / Where yellow chinkies love to play / In Limehouse / Where you can hear those blues all day.*

In *Limehouse Blues*, Anna May plays a resplendent woman, Tu Tuan, who dances for a club, the Lily Gardens, owned by her lover, a Eurasian man in yellowface. He falls for a homeless pickpocket, a white girl named Toni, housing her and ignoring all of Tu Tuan's warnings. Later in the film, Tu Tuan takes a dagger and impales herself with it.

In *Shanghai Express*, Anna May plays a woman riding a train to Shanghai. In a penultimate scene, she finds a dagger and murders Warner Oland in yellowface. She and her knife are inseparable, like lovers!

Are you ready to go to the Eighth Square now? Anna May asks. The oar in my hand has turned into Anna May's dagger.

Queen Alice

In the world of fashion, China is a land in which postmodernity finds its natural expression. Several artifacts featured in "Enigmatic Objects" reflect multiple meanderings of Orientalist influences between East and West. Perhaps the most compelling are the examples of blue-and-white porcelain. Developed in Jingdezhen, China, during the Yuan dynasty (1271–1368) blue-and-white porcelain was exported to Europe as early as the sixteenth century.

Emerging from the silver-screen nightmare, we float back into the exhibition. A Ming vase, a Ming vase gown. Chinese blue-and-white wares, precious for centuries, porcelains that divined the fates of empires. Cobalt was the only material that could withstand the heat of ancient kilns.

Channel the cobalt's endurance in order to fulfill your mission, says Anna May. *Even if you burn alive, you have to prevail. Look at me. I've died so many times—stabbed to death, torched in a fire, drowned in the ocean. If they kill me, so what? We fight beyond the grave.*

Porcelain burns for hours, glows in glaze, lasts for centuries, turns brittle. The surface of the vase is smooth—the blue depicts a temple, a willow much like the one that sang, and a bridge. She continues: *To be a Queen is to be a firebrand. Branded with fire, like this porcelain vase, you will grow armor. Your blisters arm you with knowledge. Touch this vase and they will disappear.* I touch the willow. The blue welts on my hand shrink into cicatrices. Shame brands scar tissue into the shape of stars.

These scars look marvelous, don't you agree? Stitch a new garment out of it! The Red Queen marches through the doorway. *You've reached the Eighth Square. It's time we dress you.* Together the Red Queen and the White Queen slip a blue china gown by Guo Pei over my head. It's the most exquisite garment I've ever seen. The gown's pleats resemble plates, a train of blue flowers. Wearing it, I am several centuries wiser. A crown appears on my head, scalding names into my skull. And the dagger I have turns into a scepter in disguise.

You are borne of earth and fire, says the Red Queen. *Now it's time to slay.*

You'll enter the Dinner Party with your enemies, Queen Alice, says the White Queen.

Here I go on my suicide mission. Blessed by the Queens, I am ready.

Shaking

By embracing the other, their clothes, like those depicted in eighteenth- and nineteenth-century Orientalist paintings, fabricate an alternative identity through a process of self-displacement. Postcolonial discourse perceives an implicit power imbalance in such Orientalist dress up, but designers' intentions often lie outside such rationalist cognition. They are driven less by the logic of politics than by that of fashion, which typically pursues an aesthetic of surfaces rather than an essence governed by cultural contextualization.

In the final square, there is a tower. Past the inner sanctum, a sign: Queen Alice's Ball. A flame-faced man sits on a throne made of crossed legs. At his feet, two Major Arcana cards. The center cards are Death (the thirteenth trump) and The Tower (the sixteenth trump). The man is the King, the Autocrat, the Head of State. He shits in a toilet made of gold. In his chambers, handmaidens bathe his feet.

I can do anything to them, he boasts, like Scheherazade's King, who beheaded the virgins. Beside him are a suite of men with all the power to invent but no imagination. They are discontent. Their masculinity broils in tubs of lard.

I enter the hallway—my incisors go soft. My bones turn rubbery, my skull turns brittle, and everywhere I itch—my skin no longer serves me, does not protect me from the outside environment. Where is my stealth? Where is my celerity?

The scepter turns back. With the White Queen's dagger, I rip into the King. I tear out the insides of him, but instead of intestines, there is stuffing. He has no beating organs. He continues to laugh. He cannot die. No matter how hard I stab, no matter how I try to eviscerate, I cannot find his vitals—he is like a relic of a dodo from the Museum of Natural History. I try shaving off his hair, I can't find his roots. I try sawing at his neck, slip my blade into his contusion, but no blood gushes out. No nerves, no muscle, no tissue, no blood. No blood.

Waking

I can't explain

the psychic
experience of living

inside this body
this panopticon

All I do is brace
myself

Which Dreamed It?

Rather than censor or disregard depictions of cultural others that are not wholly accurate, it advocates studying these representations on their own terms, appreciating them from the outset as having been infused with imagination and discovering in this complex dialogue of elided or transfigured meanings, a unified language of shared signs.

Back at the exhibition hall, on one of the screens, men in metal headdresses march across an open square. It's a scene from *The Last Emperor*, a film by the Italian director Bernardo Bertolucci, released in 1987. The boy emperor's face is projected onto the twin walls of a hallway of chromatic screens. Visitors take selfies in front of these projections of undulating light, their faces drowned in the pores of his young face. Between the film projections of *The Curse of the Golden Flower* and *Farewell My Concubine*, I wake from my dream.

In the threshold between maker and muse and beholder, a power axis persists. In his 1972 film *Last Tango in Paris*, Bertolucci plotted to film a young girl's real horror during her rape scene. He coveted her humiliation. He coveted it so much he decided to surprise her with it.

And if art transgresses the boundaries of artifice? And if reverie reels in reality?

Who dreamed that world I waded through? In *Through the Looking-Glass*, it was the Red King who dreamed the world all along, not Alice. He was the ruler, the wizard, and he loved to look, so the world stretched for him, made him a Palace, a Kingdom, and then a Wonderland. They multiplied his eyes, mass-produced his pupils that drink everything. Then they hid these eyes in every pore of every plant, every hidden camera in every dressing room of every daughter, princess, Queen.

That evening after leaving the museum, I go into Central Park. Dazed, I walk along the reservoir. Sometimes people fish here and I've seen their lures search for mouths under the membrane of water. Sometimes a turtle climbs over the lily pads. Sometimes a weed blooms at my feet. I throw my robe up. It floats over the reservoir like a silk moth. It doesn't sink.

Inside the kiln of history, a porcelain chest drum burns, beats, breaks. We tread on, frail and frayed and afraid as we are, to a kingdom with a better imagination. Silkworms always die for human imagination. It's a miracle that I am wild. Silk moths know only captivity and survival is the exception.

The properties of porcelain: strength / Hardness
Grit / Durability / Resilience / Long the property
of the rich / Seal of royals / Long plundered
Long looted / Long lived / Long displayed
in the pantries of private residences
If the Royal British Army sacks a
City / Breaks the glass / Ransacks
Treasures / Rapes the women
and transports the art / To
the Buckingham Palace,
Is that what they mean
by *civilization*? / In the Met,
a plate with the VOC monogram,
the Dutch East India Company / Luxury
goods on Sotheby's / Gourmet tea, colonialism
Opium shoved down the throats of the derelict
Bodies destroyed over and over for the sanctity
of capital / Is that what / They mean / By *peace*?
Looted Benin bronzes / Crackle-glazes and celadons
The Jade head of a goddess, captive for centuries / Do
we dare wish / For freedom / A chimera, part tiger,
part panther / Mouth, snout, a set of eyes / Forged
from fury always   Another property
of porcelain: High resistance
to thermal shock   Chemical attack
One year into the pandemic / In Atlanta,
a white man shoots / Kills eight people
Most were Asian women / He regards
not as "people" but "temptations" / As a
policeman parrots his words to the press
Daily the people on the streets risk the cold
The tear gas / The pandemic / The police / To ask
a nation: *Do you want to protect people or your property?*
Ask the cops: *Who exactly do you serve? Who do you protect?*
Not the people / But the prisons / The pipelines / The fences

We march / For Black liberation / For Indigenous land and water
America / We march / An uprising / To vitrify is to transform
We become the chimera forged in fire / Sum of a long summer
Long simmer / Long rage / Dear chimera / Tonight we dream

Haibun: Spring

Spring turns to summer, hopes fly high. A golden romance—in my bloody fists I smell sweet osmanthus flowers. In my hope for honey, I drink wolfberry tea, which my mother recommends for ruddy health. Under the pulped sun, lovers grow young and younger. Everyone kisses inside empty school buses, everyone says goodbye. Cheekbones that bruise outside incandesce inside. I can't stop sobbing in bed alone or with another. Riding bikes next to the lake, hold my hands under the bridge. The first time it touches me, the pink blossom revolts me. Winter stripped the willow bark bare. We pray the leaves will grow back. I can't read the names carved on the tree—who are they? Did they survive?

Under the sun, lovers are revolting. Hunger strike—all food tastes like poison. Nurses in uniforms bring us IVs. We are all fainting. Is it starvation? Is it rage? Tear gas with its peppery odor touches the petals falling across my thighs. My knee-high socks, my school uniform, my nosebleed. The chants grow louder and louder, the squadrons whistle. Batons, holsters, handcuffs, and then martial law. The screams, the spring, the safety line. *Don't forget to drink water,* my mother tells me. *Don't forget your wolfberry tea.* She begs me not to go, but I go.

my hands are up, lungs
full of fish, I drop my phone
into the lake

Chimera

Lion-headed woman, prowling
in penumbra—your goat's body, spry
and sleek, unmatched, your serpent's
tail, vestigial, why have you lost
all hope? A vestige of your follies,
fancies, the candied dreams you once
harbored and ate with ardor,
now bittering the bottom
of your chipped porcelain cup.
For years you've wandered, braving
high altitudes and rising seas, in search
of a place to anchor your impossible dreams.
You wanted love, romance. You wanted a family.
You wanted justice and truth and all of it.
You, so improbable that even your mother
marveled: *how on earth could a creature
like* you *begin in my womb?*
And she laughed, and you laughed,
but the sting passed through your body
like a season or a lover never to be heard
from again. Barnum's ad for the Feejee
Mermaid shows three nude sirens
with flowing blonde hair—his heavenly
hoax: a mummified half monkey, half fish,
ribs knotted like ropes around a sinking mast.
She has haunted museums for centuries,
promising beauty, promising wonder,
then giving us a hirsute face so ugly
it feels revolutionary. This year, scientists
have created the first chimeric embryos:
half human, half monkey, destined to
cease existing beyond a few miraculous

cells. A new technology of monsters,
the genetic possibilities bottomless.
Lion-headed woman, if your chimera
was forged and colored in fire, let it touch
air to vitrify so you know it's real.
And if it is broken, or stolen from you
once, twice, fifty times, I promise
it will come back, feathered and fleshed,
a white peach fuzzing its cold red lips.

a dream or a fox

After Lucille Clifton

plane landing in berlin, i saw a fox
      on the tarmac

beneath the wind, the fuselage,
      its eyes barbed like concertina

wire. was it a dream i do not know
      and dangerously, i took
it as a sign my ache would end.

      it didn't, but that's
okay. what would we all give
for moments like that: pure hope

materializing on the bodies
      of animals we've seen lurching
in those places they don't belong,

how they refuse to recede,
      how they hold on,
proving every human wrong.

Playing Dead

The first time I was touched,

parts of me were seen:
the nautilus, the teeth,

the cavern of mouth, how a question
marks the spine and then it is never

answered
how his seeing became my seeing,

and he surprised me, his finger
slipped into

a barren—burrows
a bare

contusion,
I thought I was exposed

but unbeknownst to me,
most parts remained unseen

and I was to retain this unseen feeling
for most of my life,
I've spent apart, not a part

of any tribe or religion or posse,
most of my life I identified with animals

like the possum
searching for trash or playing dead.

After this thing was done to me,
I believed I played a part in it,

like how an actress finds a part
so she could slip, finally, into another skin,
my parts, these parts—

I wrote the whole thing
off, my feelings were leaves
that bypassed everyone and buried me.

In autumn, my seams parted
and all I did was write a poem—an ode
to roadkill

and a decade passed before I knew
I didn't give

permission, the only thing I could control
was my reaction: wide-eyed, limp,
maybe a gasp, maybe a sigh.

When the possum plays dead, it enters
a shock stage.

It plays such a convincing part
that people have discovered possums this way
and buried them alive.

Comatose, its glands produce rotting scents,
green mucus shrouding its body
to repel predators.

The laws of predation know
a carcass can't be harmed

the same way a living thing can:
even a predator is afraid of a dead
body in the dark.

And then the possum lies still
on an empty road, under stars or pine trees
she'll never see,

until eventually a car comes speeding down the highway
and kills her, this time for real.

The Birth of Venus

Born again, killed again,
drowned in motherless
pearl. Mothers all dying
without the sheen they took
for granted. Love the queen
conch for how she houses her own
sacral insides, furious gloss
pink and slick with living
flesh. Animal, you are doomed
to lay your sticky eggs in the dust,
kneel before your beauty
until it smites you, grabs you
by your hair and drags. *Just this once*,
you pray to your ancestors, and refuse
to be evicted from your helix
and spirals. You live inside a murex
shell. It withstands the ocean,
which never bothers to shelter
its most tender tenants.

The Peony Pavilion

In the concrete garden, he appears.
Before long I'm holding his hand.
We are in Hangzhou, walking the length

of the famous lake. He is a young scholar
in a full cotton robe. We kiss under the willows,

then he pulls down my pants against the pink
pagoda wall. The cameras watch.
It happens so fast. It's getting dark already.

Dank. The water under the bridge
rips, red. At West Lake, sunset makes

us sweat like horses. The famous opera
originating here is about a woman who turns
into a snake: *The White Maiden Locked*

for Eternity in the Leifeng Pagoda.
I think of a girl from another opera

who meets a phantasmic suitor in a dream.
In the garden of rotten roses they meet, part.
She pines and pines, then dies from longing.

At a bar called Peony, my friend confesses
that most intimacy in her life she has never

fully consented to. Can intimacy be forced?
Sometimes I submit to someone else's desires
to fulfill my perceived function to them,

which is bleak. She drinks from her mojito
and laughs. Men bump into her on purpose,

trying to flirt. I want to stand on the stool and spill
tequila on their scalps. The kindest men are always

the ones in operas. Or the ones I make up,
dream of. I always wake up. But I'm not willing
to die from that disappointment.

Romance of the Castle-Toppler

The castle-toppler is one word for a woman

> or more literally: a kingdom-destroying concubine—

> n. *woman who brings about the downfall of an empire*
> v. *to cause a city or state's collapse*

In Chinese she is qingcheng, in Japanese she is kisei—

> 红颜祸水

> red face, troubled water,

> a dangerous beauty who rains ruin upon the nation.

翼

The castle-toppler originates in excess.

Sometimes she is a concubine and other times a vagrant. One rumor says she is a comb sister who at ten, swears she'd never marry, marks her oath with a mulberry stain.

Sometimes she is a goddess, but no one worships her. People spit on her shrines, leave moldy flowers.

In the flesh, she is dead and has been dead for some time. Her bones give away to mycelium kingdoms. Wildflowers cover her limbs. Heather and heart's ease. Mushrooms feast on her body, worms feast on the fungus, birds feast on the worms.

And when the dawn arrives and the foxes find the birds, breaking their necks, the woman has already been buried deep inside another instrument of hollow bones.

妹

The first known record of a woman earning the title
of "castle-toppler" is Moxi, 末喜, imperial concubine

of King Jie, a tyrant who oppressed his people, but all his bad behaviors
were attributed to his consort—facile woman facing west

the legend goes, Moxi bathed in a lake full of red wine,
laughing at men who drowned, drunk, in its carnal

depths. Moxi loved the sound of silks tearing, so every day
new bolts arrived from the north, ripped apart

for her pleasure—laying waste to silkworms,
the women weavers, doom spelled on their looms.

妹

The castle-toppler lives in the text.

In the text, she is inviolable in the sense that her body cannot be penetrated. A
surface, a sheet.

She is imagined but never touched. It's safer that way.

If this simulacrum begins to consume her, she can slip the knife to the silk screen
and end it.

There are so many stories she could put an end to. Because the text, like skin,
also ends.

妹

Examples of castle-topplers:

Bao Si (褒姒): the concubine of Emperor You of Zhou. Bao Si was the daughter of a slave girl bewitched by a lizard. It was an immaculate conception.

Daji (妲己): the concubine of Emperor Zhou of Shang. Considered one of history's most evil women, possessed by a nine-tailed fox demon.

Xi Shi (西施): one of the Four Great Beauties of history in the Zhou. Used as a honey trap for King Fuchai of Wu and a spy for her kingdom.

Zhao Feiyan (趙飛燕): the concubine of Emperor Cheng of Han. Rose to become Empress Xiaocheng.

Yang Yuhuan (楊玉環): the concubine of Emperor Xuanzong of Tang. Scapegoated for her kingdom's failings.

罪

Before she becomes a castle-toppler, she was a comb sister, and before that, she was an imperial silk-weaver.

At the silk factory, she spins her hair on her loom—her love scalped, she is already monstrous.

She plucks out the wolfberry and its gold seeds smeared her sleeve. She eats the nub, the bark. She wants to believe in the beauty of sericulture, of the future.

Her sisters comb their hair, part it sideways to promise a lifetime of celibacy.

A silkworm threads its cocoon over and over, an eternal maiden.

Inside the cocoon, the pupa is boiled alive.

Has it given up on moth-hood, like these comb sisters give up motherhood?

The pact she makes to avoid that one common mistake—marriage, mulberry bruises, stains on white dresses from excess drinking, excess dreaming.

狐

In the beginning of *Romance of the Three Kingdoms*, the emperor asks his counsel to explain the calamities and marvels that have befallen his kingdom. His minister answers: *Falling rainbows and changes of bird fowl's sexes are brought about by the interference of empresses and eunuchs in state affairs.*

If beauty signaled *so* much power, why did four out of four historical beauties die tragically?

Xi Shi, rumored to drown in a lake where the fish once drowned in awe of her beauty.

Yang Yuhuan, whose beauty made flowers wilt in shame, rumored to strangle herself in front of a Buddhist shrine by the decree of her husband, the emperor.

Wang Zhaojun, whose beauty caused birds to fall to their deaths, wanted to go home, but she, a political bride, was forever exiled in the West, rumored to die at thirty-three of homesickness, buried in a tomb of clean spring grass.

Diaochan, whose beauty made the moon wane in shame, rumored to stab herself with the seven-star dagger.

狐

The castle-toppler rides the gale of justice with her rare fowl feathers.

She is a fowl, fouling the borders. She swims to escape her princes.

She is the empress of calamities and marvels.

Weakened by rumors and snakebites, the castle-toppler writes hundreds of poems steeped in the juice of indigo plants.

Inside the walls, palace intrigue. The empress and consorts send herbal decoctions, cyanide powder.

In the world outside, they teach her what to want, how to want it.

Sleep, they tell her. You must sleep for beauty. You must sleep to not grow old. You must sleep for many years, eat only wolfberries and peaches. Ripen.

眠

In Xi'an, I scaled the walls at the Chang'an South Gate,
the origin of the Silk Road. Under its eaves,

I overhear a performance: "The Song of Everlasting
Sorrow," the story of Yang Yuhuan, a spectacular tragedy.

The lights from the show rakes the autumn
sky. For a moment, I want to die

for love too. I have never felt that sentiment
returned. As the rebellion turned to insurrection,

Yang Yuhuan could not flee her kingdom. Her love
ordered her to die, so she obeyed.

I have never lived a sorrow
that deep. To romanticize history
is to forget it. That's the privilege of nostalgia.

眠

In her Kingdom of Self, the castle-toppler sleeps for many years.

In slumber, she is happy. Rabbit rains, a silk-spun sky. Foxes climb her shadows, lick her ankles.

The castle-toppler has a flowery dream of revenge: late at night, the palace lit with fireflies. The revenge in the osmanthus forest smells sweet, earthy. A perfumed and honeyed poison in the air.

And when she awakens, a prince sits by her bedside, staring at her.

She gathers her wits, her skirts, and she screams.

The scream lasts for two days, two nights. The scream lasts through the typhoon warnings. The scream lasts through the typhoon and its aftermath. Rain pelts down the castle, casting a luminous shadow over the windows. The prince covers his ears. The prince's throat is a snuff box to launch the torch song into.

羿

Zhao Feiyan, the fifth historical beauty (demoted for her questionable motives), killed herself while tomb-sweeping.

After uprisings in her kingdom, Moxi was exiled and died in shame and suffering.

Bao Si hung herself during a siege.

Daji executed by the state.

What's the Han dynasty expression?

红颜薄命

Beautiful women suffer tragic fates—

With great beauty comes great ruin!

꟱

Once I entered the palace I understood
that nothing was mine I was another bride
with no face   just a debauched
existence   to replace
another debauched existence
that to survive   I had to climb
the ranks   palace lady   noble consort
                              imperial concubine
and give birth   to a son of Heaven
that the empress will poison me
or frame me for drowning   my own child
that the emperor plucked me from my impoverished life
and I had to be grateful
for his cruelty
for the rest of my life   that the pavilions
and plum blossoms were all tinged cherry
from hungry ghosts who are really
just out for blood   that women of my rank
flung themselves over the painted palace eaves
that the view here was truly
to die for
that material comforts meant
there were no boundaries of what someone
could do to me   it's dog eat dog
and every eunuch for himself   and really
I am lonely at dawn   in the silks
of a lie and   someone else's dream

꟱

When the prince finally returns, she is nowhere to be found. Only poems remain.

She climbs out, she swims in the moat that she mistakes for the sea. The prince cries out.

In a moat of scum, the castle-toppler lets her prince drown. It is not regicide, per se.

In the scholar's gardens of pale camellias and sweet osmanthus, the castle-toppler plants skunk onions.

Bird's eye chilis to turn the mouths of men into silent holes for her probing, leave them without tongue or dominion.

The castle-toppler rips the chasm open, lets all empires burn.

The Belladonna of Sadness

Spring in Hell and everything's blooming.

I dreamt the worst was over but it wasn't.

Suppose my punishment was fields of lilies sharper than razors, cutting up fields of lies.

Suppose my punishment was purity, mined and blanched.

They shunned me only because I knew I was stunning.

Then the white plague came, and their pleas were like a river.

Summer was orgiastic healing, snails snaking around wrists.

In heat, garbage festooned the sidewalks.

Old men leered at bodies they couldn't touch

until they did. I shouldn't have laughed but I laughed

at their flesh dozing into their spines, their bones crunching like snow.

Once I was swollen and snowblind with grief, left for dead

at the castle door. Then I robbed the castle and kissed my captor,

my sadness, learned she was not a villain. To wake up in this verdant field,

to watch the lilies flay the lambs. To enter paradise,

a woman drinks a vial of amnesia. Found in only the palest

flowers, the ones that smell like rotten meat. To summon the stinky

flower and access its truest aroma, you have to let its stigma show.

You have to let the pollen sting your eyes until you close them.

I will never dance for you

Hunting is a cocksure rite of passage
Hurting is the origin of everything

May they rip you or ripen you / Remove the bullets and tell me what you find

My quitting / I quit the search party / I quit the chase / I quit the object of my affliction

I quit the floor / I quit the sit-in / I quit the tiny room with the spring mattress

I quit spring and summer and fall and winter / I quit

I quit the plums shriveling in their own liquids / I quit the quince trees in the yard next door

I quit the wolfberry tea that prolongs my vanity

I quit the bunting formation heading swiftly toward the sea

I quit the spit in my mouth / I quit the throb and the sob and the yelp and the yowl

I quit the wilderness / I quit the story with its arms cut off

Good girls can't
Good girls can't be gods / You wanted me wet but not awake

Come at me / Come starve me / These ribs these legs this hotbed of knots
On my shoulders this cursive curse / You want to grip and grope

When we make a racket out of sweat / When we twist our parts

You restrain me / Gild and geld me/ When I shudder / You shutter

You erect fences / You erect

Borders / Your erectile missive / Laying claim to my horror

Try to train me to obey / My borders / Make me kneel / Make me spend

All the moneyshots / Until we are spent / Until we are nothing

I've got nothing for you / So fuck you

This dance / Taunts you with my aliveness / My wretchedness / You push me against a wall
Lean in / Gnaw my ear / I tear up untorn / My penumbra glows / My crown turns blue

Regal with rage / And I won't dance, motherfucker

I won't dance for you

Minted

—Anna May Wong is the first Asian American woman
to appear on the US quarter dollar, 2022

O, to be the face of money! 2022: newly
minted, you are a new woman. The face
of capital. The face of lucre. Preface:

your nails tapping against IN GOD
WE TRUST. But he is heads, you are tails.
Toss a coin for the chance of it being you

or George Washington. It's always George.
George and his bloodhounds. George, father
of a republic, patriarch of this nation you died

in. In life, so many people thought it was okay
to discard you. And they did—that director,
his lewd smile, how he put his hand behind

your ear. You were sixteen, seventeen. That was
how you were assessed: a girl doll, forever
foreign, stupid flower, spoiled with one touch.

How we've grown used to being used once, expend-
able. You, me, pretty commodities: fungible,
fungal, funny, fun. Fun! But for whom? No glory

to girlhood or Hollywood. No glory to money
or matrimony. Nation or state. Treasure, treasury,
treachery. Tell us, fathers, have we come very far?

Your father was a laundry man. Every day of his life,
he encountered stains. A century later, I drag
my linens to the laundromat, trade dollars for coins

with your face on them. Each new quarter dreams
another cycle inside this machine of cleanness.
But none of my dresses are in mint condition.

Some stains I cherished, some stains I wanted
gone. For this coin, I watch my stains tumble,
obedient to the laws of disappearance.

American Loneliness

I used to be proud of not conforming to stereotypes, such as: meek, submissive Asian woman

I used to relish the startled looks of street harassers when I talk back

To the white man who groped me on a drawbridge in Ithaca, I said *I'm going to murder you*

That feral night in 2011, there were no stones to pelt him with

But when he started sprinting in the opposite direction, I chased after him, because if he was so dangerous, why would he run away?

No one cares about your pathetic fetish, why don't you go fuck yourself with a dollar-store Fleshlight

That year, I met a woman whose husband called her a "Chinese maid"

I wondered if this man even knew that the woman he married was the recent head of a medical school department

A futile reflex: to list someone's credentials as a plea to be treated with respect

Because if she *was* a maid, he'd probably make even more jokes at her expense

She was an immigrant, she didn't get these jokes and so laughed along with him

I can't count the number of men who put on their dating profiles: *I'm looking for a woman who doesn't take herself seriously* or *I want a woman who can laugh at herself*

Googling *why straight men only want to date women who don't take themselves seriously* yields some answers: *because life is too short, because*

But life is long sometimes, and humiliation inevitable

In 2016, the first Chinese American woman was crowned Miss Michigan, would compete in the next Miss America

She ran on the platform "Being American: Immigration & Citizenship Education"

Mobs of people on the Internet called her ugly

In a video interview titled "Miss Michigan reads nasty comments people make, and she is 'thankful' for them," Miss Michigan says, *You can think I'm ugly and that's fine, but I want to talk about the things that are important*

I used to be ashamed of how the Asian stereotype meant: docile and accommodating, conformist, collectivist, faceless, generic, robotic, never complaining, eager to be exploited, taking mistreatment just as a fact of life

And I was so eager to be different because being the same was not an option

Not all "firsts" are great firsts—more often, to be the "first" is to face uncharted humiliation

For example, the first Chinese women to immigrate to San Francisco were sold in the barracoons as sex slaves, their naked bodies probed by strangers and appraised

For example, the first documented person to die of COVID-19 was a sixty-one-year-old man who loved going to the seafood market on Saturdays to buy dried squid

And that's how this city, my birthplace, became a household name—Wuhan, the first epicenter of a deadly pandemic

Days into the Wuhan lockdown, one headline read: "*Outcasts* in their own country, the people of Wuhan are the *unwanted* faces of China's coronavirus outbreak"

After being kicked out of her guesthouse in Changsha, one woman sat on a park bench and watched the sun set over the Xiangjiang River

It was the Spring Festival, she was heading back home from college with seaweed snacks and zongzi in her backpack

All over China, stranded Hubei tourists dreamt of shelter

Within three months, Wuhan recovered with a strict lockdown and contact tracing

Meanwhile, America reels

Three hundred seventy days into the pandemic, another massacre takes place in Atlanta

The killer was a white man whose sex addiction made him view Asian women as "temptations" which, according to him, "wasn't a race thing"

In another instance, security camera footage showed a sixty-five-year-old woman shoved, punched, and kicked in front of 360 West 43rd Street

"Fuck you! You don't belong here!" the man shouted, kicking her on the head over and over

On January 15th, 2022, a forty-year-old Asian woman was pushed and killed in front of an R train in the Times Square station

On February 13th, 2022, a thirty-five-year-old Asian woman was followed up six stories of her Chinatown apartment building and stabbed to death in her own home

Are we easy targets because the perception is we carry cash and don't fight back?

In the Bay Area, an Asian woman was shot in the head with a flare gun

My grandmother doesn't leave her Sunnyvale apartment anymore for fear of pathogens and hate crimes

I've always called these places home—the Bay Area, New York City—but now

Home teaches us to be more vigilant / more afraid

If that Ithaca man had groped me now, ten years later, would I dare chase him down the street?

Maybe the desire to say "I'm from America" is the desire to distance myself from Chinese humility, Chinese humiliation

After all, China named a whole century after its humiliation

And America prides itself on exceptionalism and individualism and genius and freedom from responsibilities such as helping each other stay alive

Elon Musk with his face like a muskrat, the musketeer of the apocalyptic space dildo

Jeff Bezos in his ugly tight pants and clown face

Elizabeth Holmes in her blood money Issey Miyake turtleneck on the cover of *Fortune* with the headline "Out for Blood"

My mother used to work as a scientist in Elizabeth Holmes's company, drank the "Silicon Valley wunderkind" Kool-Aid

Theranos was funded with blood money—Henry Kissinger on the board

All through college I heard stories about how Elizabeth, the twenty-two-year-old blonde, was the most enterprising Stanford prodigy

Toward the end of her time there, my mother worked long, unforgiving hours at the lab developing assays for the Edison, that miracle blood-test machine

Sometimes she'd stay in the lab until 2a.m. with no paid overtime

When given the choice to take a pay raise or stocks, my mother opted for the stocks

She was let go after she expressed doubts about the machine's readiness for the general public

And when the company spiraled, my mother spiraled with it and lost everything

Perhaps American exceptionalism is really just American loneliness

My mother said that working like this is just a fact of life in Silicon Valley, her exploitation is not an exception

Why do we aspire to prove ourselves as American if this is what we know about it?

Five hundred days into a pandemic, Elizabeth Holmes is playing with her wolf-dog Balto outside her fancy condo in San Francisco, pregnant and engaged to the heir of a hotel fortune

Perhaps the American dream is an American gag order / American gag reflex / American gag

Joke's on us / The jig is up / I'm drowning in the gig economy, a mouthful of sores

I've voted and voted and voted and voted and still nothing

American dream / American exception / American exceptionalism exempts us from looking outward / Into the sky through our masks / Exempts us from looking inward too

In 1999 I learned that American beauty is a blonde teen in a rose petal bathtub willing to fuck a middle-aged man

In 2002 the popular T-shirts for preteen girls said "princess," as if the most famous princess of the time hadn't been emotionally abused in front of the entire world before dying tragically in a freak car accident

In 2008 I learned who America bailed out in a financial crisis

In 2009 I learned that American success is a blonde teen dropping out of Stanford

The kind of capitalism we live under: zombifying hope / cannibalizing desire / mummifying pain

Another winter in this pandemic and I am back to this drawing board

Almost a million dead and the government telling us to "deal with it"

Small apartment, hissing heater, untouched body, short breaths

At-home rapid tests cost $25 / A box of masks costs $15 / A PCR test costs $125 at private clinics

American dream / American solitude / American isolation / American loneliness

Or American hopelessness

It is January 4th, 2022, and Elizabeth Holmes has been found guilty of defrauding billionaire investors such as the DeVos family

But not guilty of defrauding patients—no justice for the woman whose faulty blood test told her she would miscarry

It is January 6th, 2022, and the first snowfall of winter transformed Manhattan overnight

Anniversary of an attempted insurrection by militant white supremacists on the Capitol

Schools reopening for the spring as hospitals overfill

Salted trash bags heaped with brand new snow, all tinseled

Remains: pistachio shells, a stained carpet, a fractured mirror, a triple-bladed fan

On February 4th, the Beijing Winter Olympics commenced, and flocks of American journalists call their COVID safety precautions "dystopic"

"Dystopic": the robot spraying the hotel lobby with Lysol, a man serving cocktails in full PPE, the safety precautions to keep us all from dying

On May 17th, we surpass one million dead from COVID in America

On June 24th, the Supreme Court abolishes *Roe v. Wade* with *Dobbs v. Jackson* and I can't stop thinking about my mother

How she came here on a gamble for that old cliché, "freedom"

On this sunny day in Chinatown, I walk by Kimlau Square on my way to the Silk Road Café

The arch towering over me says "In Memory of the Americans of Chinese Ancestry Who Lost Their Lives In Defense of Freedom and Democracy"

And there in the shadow of this monument I noticed that the American obsession with freedom is the American obsession with death

I wonder where that Wuhan woman is now, years after she threw her wish into the river, panicked about the encroaching night

Wherever she is now, I hope she's safe and warm

Haibun: Kintsugi

Gold in the cracks. Thank god the vase was broken. Why did I believe that repair would never mend it back to its beauty? Over the years, mending has become a monotony.

Never mind the slow burn of a porcelain birth—the million live embers, extinguished. Heat quelled: this was what it was, to live. Existing, carrying so much emptiness, unable to hold water.

To soak the shattered bits overnight in whole milk. To repair an ewer with precious metals. A little gold leaf, a little honey, don't be afraid, let its fractures show. A history of pain as clear as spring water running over the legs.

Apply adhesive—
pinch of gold, silver of ash.
She was broken, thank
god.

On Garbage

Every day on the back of our '89 Mitsubishi Galant,
I searched the curbs for precious garbage.

It was the 90s, my parents were scraping by,
and I learned to sharpen this vigilance—
pay attention to what everyone throws away.

Our first three TVs, our first couch, our first coffee
table, its glass crackled, its oak rough,
how I learned to love garbage

because it gave me hope
to rescue what was abandoned,
what was beyond repair.

Eight years old, I was home alone too much.
No story had to end in the dumpster.
I prized even the broken things: the TV sets

with bent antennas, the moth-eaten lace, the paperbacks
dropped in bathwater. Then I learned shame.

What if I had known then what I know now—
that landfills, like churches and streets, have names.

The largest landfills in America have pleasant
ones: Pine Tree Acres, Sunshine Canyon.
And some have terrible names, like Fresh Kills

on Staten Island, once a salt flat, then a tidal strait,
a dump, then finally a park. The trash mounds capped
in clean soil, like snow dressing the loneliness

of summits. All the drawings I wish I'd kept,
the toys I thought I'd outgrown, the aches of girlhood.

I was wrong to think I could let it all go. My mother's
father was a hoarder, so she loved tearing things up,
throwing them out. She made a carnival of it.

Every day, the crinkling and crushing,
the tossing. Of course she'd raise a daughter
who excelled at dumpster diving.

Among the treasures I rifled out of the trash, I found
myself.

Notes

"Nucleation" and "Red Tide" respond to the life of Kōkichi Mikimoto, b. 1858, who invented the practice of culturing pearls.

"Paris Syndrome" refers to a psychological condition experienced almost exclusively by Japanese tourists and, to a lesser extent, Chinese tourists, who are disappointed when the City of Light does not live up to their romantic expectations. The syndrome, considered an extreme case of culture shock, causes symptoms such as an acute delusional state, hallucinations, anxiety, dizziness, and sweating, and has been documented by tourism offices, the Japanese Embassy in Paris, and medical journals. Single woman travelers are most afflicted by this disease.

"On Silk" quotes passages from Langston Hughes's autobiography and travelogue *I Wonder as I Wander* (Hill and Wang, 1993) in which he describes his travels to Shanghai and around the world. The Sanmao quote is from *Stories of the Sahara* (Bloomsbury Publishing, 2020). The Eileen Chang quote is from her essay "My Dream of Genius" in her essay collection *Written in Water*, translated by Andrew F. Jones (Columbia University Press, 2005).

"One Thousand Boats" uses details from Yayoi Kusama's autobiography, *Infinity Net*, translated by Ralph McCarthy (University of Chicago Press, 2012).

"The Kingdom of Surfaces" uses section titles named after chapters in Lewis Carroll's *Through the Looking-Glass*. The quotes are pulled from *China Through the Looking Glass: Fashion, Film, Art*, the book pertaining to the eponymous exhibition at the Metropolitan Museum of Art, specifically the chapter "Toward an Aesthetic of Surfaces" by Andrew Bolton (The Metropolitan Museum of Art, 2015).

"a dream or a fox" is a response poem to a suite of poems in Lucille Clifton's *the terrible stories* (BOA Editions, 1996) titled "the dream of foxes."

"The Peony Pavilion" references the Kunqu opera of the same name, written by Tang Xianzu in 1598 and put on by director Tan Dun at the Metropolitan Museum of Art in 2012.

"Romance of the Castle-Toppler" references *Romance of the Three Kingdoms*, the classical fourteenth-century novel by Luo Guanzhong.

"The Belladonna of Sadness" references the 1973 film of the same name, directed by Eiichi Yamamoto.

Acknowledgments

Huge gratitude to the following journals, whose editors published these poems in their first forms: The Academy of American Poets' *Poem-a-Day*, *The Adroit Journal*, *The American Poetry Review*, *Cero Magazine*, *Crazyhorse*, *Granta*, *Harper's Bazaar*, *The Kenyon Review*, *Literary Hub*, *Los Angeles Review of Books Quarterly*, *The Massachusetts Review*, *The New England Review*, *The New Republic*, *The Offing*, *The Paris Review*, *Poetry*, *A Public Space*, *The Rumpus*, *Split This Rock Poem of the Week*, *Tin House*, *Virginia Quarterly Review*, and *The Yale Review*.

"a dream or a fox" was commissioned by the 92nd Street Y, New York, Unterberg Poetry Center for their feature "Joy and Hope and All That: A Tribute to Lucille Clifton."

"Batshit" was published in the 2020 anthology *Together in a Sudden Strangeness: America's Poets Respond to the Pandemic*, edited by Alice Quinn.

"Loquats," first published in the *Paris Review*, was selected for inclusion in *Pushcart Prizes: Best of the Small Presses*, 2022 edition.

"Playing Dead," first published in the *Kenyon Review*, was selected for inclusion in *The Best American Poetry 2021*, edited by Tracy K. Smith.

"On Majolica" was commissioned by the Bard Graduate Center in 2021 for the exhibition *Majolica Mania: Transatlantic Pottery in England and the United States, 1850–1915*.

This book would not exist without the luminosity of my communities, mentors, colleagues, friends, and support systems. Thank you to the Dorothy and Lewis B. Cullman Center for Scholars and Writers at the New York Public Library, where I first wrote the title poem of this book. Thank you to the George Washington University Jenny McKean Writer-in-Washington program, where I began collecting more seeds. Thank you to the Black Mountain Institute at University of Nevada at Las Vegas, where I wrote many of the later poems as a Shearing Fellow in 2021. Thank you to the Swatch Art Peace Hotel and the Jerome Foundation, for the chance to research and write at an artist's residency in Shanghai, where some of these poems take place. Thank you to the Lannan Foundation's Marfa residency where I wrote some of these poems, as well as the Anderson Center in Red Wing, Minnesota. Thank you to my students and colleagues at New York University and Sarah Lawrence College.

A porcelain vase for those who have read this book in its multivarious forms: Jane Wong, Cathy Linh Che, Michael Prior, and Tarfia Faizullah. A decanter of tea for Clare Mao, my agent. A loquat tree for Anne Anlin Cheng, Terrance Hayes, and Dave Eggers, for your indispensable wisdom and conversations. A red bolt of silk for my friends who have supported me emotionally as I wrote this book: Ocean Vuong, Peter Bienkowski, Vivian Hu, Jennifer Lue, Jennifer Chang, Thora Siemsen, C. Pam Zhang, Casey Li Brander, Ricardo Maldonado, John Manuel Arias, Christopher Radcliff, Karen Gu, Aria Aber, Christopher Soto, Jia Sung, Lillian Sun, Wilson Wong, Alvin Tran, Emily Jungmin Yoon, and so many others. To my friends, near and far—*thank you.*

A string of pearls for Jeff Shotts, as always, for the incredible depth and care you put into every vision, as well as the rest of the team at Graywolf Press—Caelan Ernest Nardone, Carmen Giménez, Chantz Erolin, Katie Dublinski, Marisa Atkinson, and so many others. A special salute to Fiona McCrae, who inducted me into the Graywolf family. I can't believe how lucky I am.

To Kundiman, my forever home. To my parents, extended family, and ancestors. To past and future selves, to growth, to blossom, to art. Thank you to you, reader. To my grandparents. Here's a toast and a blessing, by my paternal grandmother Wu Juhua:

虎己归山兔己来，
上天己经做安排，
新冠病毒虎带走，
玉兔下凡送福来！
自古大疫三年止，
该与疫情说拜拜！
愿我们都能平安无恙的迎接福兔！

Sally Wen Mao is the author of two previous collections of poetry: *Oculus*, a finalist for the *Los Angeles Times* Book Prize, and *Mad Honey Symposium*. She is also the author of the short story collection *Ninetails*. The recipient of two Pushcart Prizes and a National Endowment for the Arts grant, she was a Cullman Fellow at the New York Public Library and a Shearing Fellow at the Black Mountain Institute. Her work has appeared in the *Best American Poetry*, *Granta*, *Guernica*, *Harper's Bazaar*, the *Kenyon Review*, the *Paris Review*, *Poetry*, and *A Public Space*, and elsewhere. She currently lives in New York City.

The text of *The Kingdom of Surfaces* is set in Bembo MT Pro.
Book design by Rachel Holscher.
Composition by Bookmobile Design & Digital
Publisher Services, Minneapolis, Minnesota.
Manufactured by Versa Press on acid-free,
30 percent postconsumer wastepaper.